Caring Claws

The World of Cat Moms

Shiva Kumar

COPYRIGHT

species, should educate readers about conservation, and raise awareness.

First Edition

ISBN: 978-1-963865-04-2

DEDICATION

For Sonu, whose spirit inspires every adventure within these pages.

CONTENTS

TALES FROM THE BLUE SKY

EXPLORING THE WORLD OF CARING CLAWS

I magine a huge, blue sky above a wide, golden land. The wind whispers tales of amazing cat mothers here. Welcome, everyone who loves adventure and cats! I am the sky, full of stories ready to be told. We are about to go on an exciting trip into the world of cat moms called 'Caring Claws.'

Think of floating on a cloud, flying high with me, looking down at brave cat mothers around the world. We will see green jungles, big sunny lands, and mountains covered in snow. In these beautiful places, strong cat moms, like the lioness and the snow leopard, take care of their babies with love and bravery.

Each story we discover is a treasure, teaching us about bravery, kindness, and cleverness from cat moms everywhere. Get ready for a fun journey with lots of stories, creativity, and new things to learn. With every cat sound and movement, there is something new to find out.

Are you ready to start this amazing trip into 'Caring Claws'? Hold on tight because we are about to begin an adventure! Now, imagine any cat mom you would like to meet on this journey. Let your thoughts fly as we start this exciting adventure!

Part I

Lioness, Amur Tigress, Snow Leopard, Jaguar, Cheetah, Cougar, and Eurasian Lynx

CHAPTER 1 - GUARDIANS OF THE PRIDE: THE LIONESS'S COURAGE

Introduction to Lions

W elcome to the grassy plains of Africa, where the strong lion lives.

This animal is known as the "King of the Jungle" because of its powerful look and the beautiful mane that looks like a crown. When we see lions, we are amazed by how royal and majestic they are.

Lions: Built Strong

Lions are made to be leaders in the wild. They have powerful muscles and sharp claws that help them hunt, and their golden fur blends in with the grass. Their strong bodies show they are great hunters and deserve respect from other animals.

Lionesses Lead the Way

Female lions, called lionesses, are the real heroes of the lion family. They hunt for food and take care of everyone. Lionesses are good at working together, helping each other find food and teaching their babies how to live in the wild. They also make strong friendships, which keep their family, called a pride, together and strong.

Lions in Danger

Lions used to live in many places in Africa and Asia, but now they have fewer places to live and face many dangers. We need to protect these amazing animals and the places they live in to keep nature healthy. Their lower numbers remind us that we must work hard to take care of animals like lions.

The Lion Family: Together Strong

In the open lands of Africa, lions are one of the best family groups in the wild. This family, the pride, has everyone working together, from moms and dads to the little cubs. Lionesses are the stars because they hunt, look after the babies, and protect the family.

Everyone Has a Role

In a lion pride, working as a team is important. Lionesses hunt together so everyone can eat. The male lion, who is the leader, keeps the family safe from danger. The cubs play and learn important things they need to know for when they grow up.

Silent Conversations

Lions talk to each other in their own unique way. They use roars, movements, and smells to say things like, "I am here, and this is my family." They also show love and make their family ties stronger by grooming and cuddling each other.

A Teamwork Lesson

Life in pride shows us how important it is to work together and care for each other. Lions teach us about the power of family and how to talk to each other well. They show us how to live and do well as a group.

The Hunt: A Team Effort

In the lion world, getting food is about working together. Think of the lionesses as smart hunters who sneak up on animals like zebras or buffaloes. They all have a job to do and work together like a team to hunt.

Dinner Time

After the hunt, the male lion eats first, even though the lionesses did the challenging work. Then the lionesses eat, and lastly, the cubs. This may not seem fair, but it helps the pride stay healthy.

A Wildlife

The way lions hunt and eat is a big part of their life in the wild. It shows that every lion has a place and job in the family. They all stick together, face challenges, and make sure everyone has what they need to live well.

The First Steps: Cubhood Adventures

A Secret Beginning

Lion cubs start their lives hidden away in the bush or caves, where they are born. These first moments are unique. The cubs cannot see at first and need lots of love and help from their moms.

Discovering the World

After a few weeks, the cubs start to see and want to explore everything. They might be a little shaky at first, but soon they are playing and learning about the world around them.

Learning to Be Lions

Cubs do not just play; they also learn how to be part of the pride. Their moms teach them how to hunt, find water, and know the secrets of living in the wild. They practice and learn every day.

Growing Up Brave

Growing up in the wild, cubs face many lessons and challenges. They meet new animals and learn how to be part of the pride. These experiences make them brave and ready for life in the Savannah.

A Journey of Growth

The story of a lion cub growing up is amazing. It shows us the importance of family, learning, and how each step prepares us for bigger things in life.

Protecting the King's Domain

Lions: Rulers of Their Land

Lions are like the guardians of their land. They need a lot of space for hunting and taking care of their family. They make sure other animals know this is their home by making loud noises and leaving scents.

Challenges in the Wild

Being a lion is not easy. They have less space to live because of farms and cities. There are more fights with people, and some are hunted illegally. These problems make it hard for lions to live safely.

Everyone Can Help

We can help lions! Even trivial things can make a significant difference. We can learn about lions, tell others about them, and help places that protect wild animals. By helping lions, we help many other animals and plants, too.

A Roar for the Future

The story of lions is about facing problems and working together to take care of our planet. By helping lions, we keep the wild healthy. We need to make sure lions can keep roaring in Africa for a long time.

Lions in Legend and Life

Mighty Symbols Across the Ages

Lions are not only the kings of the jungle but also stars in stories and symbols everywhere. They have been seen as strong, brave, and royal on flags and in tales since ancient times. Lions are in so many stories because they are brave and powerful.

Heroes of Myth and Legend

In old stories, lions are the brave protectors. They guard treasures and lead heroes on big adventures. They are seen as noble and keep cities and people safe. Their stories, which are old, teach us to be brave and smart.

More Than Just Strong

Lions are not just strong; they are also seen as great leaders and family members. People see how lions, in their groups called prides, work together, and take care of each other. This makes people want to be like them. Lions in art and stories show us how to be good leaders and loving family members.

Why must we protect lions?

Lions are important, not just in the wild but to us as well. They teach us about being strong, brave, and caring for each other. By protecting lions and where they live, we keep their stories and lessons alive.

The Lioness: The Pride's Superhero

The Heart and Might of the Pride

Lionesses are the superheroes of the lion world. They hunt, take care of the family, and protect everyone. They are the ones who find food, look after the babies, and keep the family safe.

Sisters Stick Together

The Lionesses are a formidable team. They share everything, from hunting to caring for the cubs. They make sure every baby is fed and safe, and they can face any challenge when they work together.

When Trouble Comes Knocking

Sometimes, a new male lion wants to take over the pride. This can be scary, but lionesses are united. They use their smarts and strength to keep their babies and pride safe. They are like supermoms to their family.

Teaching the Cubs

Lionesses also teach their babies how to live and be part of the pride. Each lesson helps prepare the cubs for the future and keeps the pride strong.

Why Lionesses Are Amazing

Lionesses show how important family is and how working together is good for everyone. They are brave and work hard, which reminds us to take care of them and their homes.

Join the Pride's Guardians

Be a Hero for Lions You can be a hero for lions from your own home. They need friends everywhere to help keep them safe. Learning about lions helps others understand why they need protection.

Fun with Lions

Create Your Pride: Make your own lion family with paper, scissors, and colors. Give each lion a job, just like in a real pride.

Walk in a Lioness's Paws: Pretend you are a lioness leading the pride. Choose how to find food, protect your cubs, and rest.

Be a Conservation Champion: Small actions help a lot. Join nature clubs, learn at the zoo, or adopt an animal online with your family.

Did you know?

Lions can roar very loudly, heard up to five miles away!

Lionesses are smart leaders in hunting and work together so the pride can eat.

Together, we can have influence

Everyone can help the lions. Talking about them, making good choices for the planet, and learning helps us protect these animals.

Our Journey with Lions: A Call to Roar Together

We learned about lions and their families and how they help each other. But lions need our help because their homes are getting smaller.

A Roar for Help

Lions' homes are disappearing, and they need heroes to protect their wild places.

Your Part in the Pride

Everyone can help lions by sharing their stories, helping wildlife, and creating art or writing about them.

Glossary

- **Lioness:** Female lions who hunt food and take care of the lion family.

- **Pride:** A family group of lions including moms, dads, and their babies.

- **Cubs:** Baby lions who learn and play under the care of their moms.

- **Hunt:** How lionesses work together to find food for their pride.

- **Roar:** The loud sound lions make to talk to each other and show their territory.

- **Territory:** The area where a lion family lives and hunts.

- **Predators:** Animals that hunt other animals for food, like lions.

- **Conservation:** Working to protect lions and their homes.

- **Carnivore:** Animals that eat meat, which includes lions.

- **Mane:** The long hair around the head of male lions.

- **Savannah:** The grassy plains in Africa where lions live.

- **Teamwork:** How lionesses work together to care for their cubs and hunt.

CHAPTER 2 - STRIPES OF RESILIENCE: THE LIFE OF THE AMUR TIGRESS

Introduction to the Amur Tigress

Majestic Stripes in the Wild

Deep in the forest, where it is quiet and nature is all around, the Amur Tigress is the most important animal.

She has a beautiful orange coat with big black stripes and moves quietly like a shadow. She is strong and uses her claws and teeth to catch food.

A Realm of Snow and Forest

The Amur Tigress lives in a place with green forests and cold snowy lands. She is good at living in both quiet places and in storms. This shows she is particularly good at surviving in her home.

Young readers, let us learn about the life of the Amur Tigress. She is a beautiful and strong animal with many secrets. We will see the wild through her eyes.

The Amur Tigress's Domain: Territory and Behavior

Guardian of the Forest

The Amur Tigress walks through the forest and shows she is the boss. She keeps her home safe by making sure everyone knows it is hers. She lives alone and is the ruler of her land.

A Life of Solitude

The Amur Tigress likes to be alone, different from lions or cheetahs that live in groups. She hunts by herself and takes care of her babies on her own. She is strong and smart, living by herself.

Whispers in the Wilderness

The Amur Tigress does not just roar; she also uses body movements and leaves signs to talk to other tigers. This is how she shows she is in charge, finds a friend, or teaches her babies.

In her home, the Amur Tigress shows us how to be strong by ourselves and teaches us the power of being quiet in nature.

Hunting Strategies and Feeding Habits

The Silent Stalker

When it starts to get dark, the Amur Tigress becomes quiet and gets ready to catch her food. She is very patient and fast. She hides with her stripes and waits for the right time to catch an animal.

The Dance of Predator and Prey

The Amur Tigress must be very skilled at catching different animals like deer or wild boar. Hunting is hard, but she is the best at it in the forest.

Feast of the Forest

After she catches an animal, the Amur Tigress eats her food. This is important for her and keeps the forest full of life. She sometimes eats a lot and sometimes a little, just like in nature.

From the Amur Tigress, we learn how the hunter and the hunted live together, keeping the forest alive.

Maternal Commitment: The Amur Tigress as a mother

A Sanctuary in the Shadows

When it is time to have babies, the Amur Tigress finds a secret place. Her babies are born small and need a lot of help. This secret place becomes important for the new cubs.

Lessons of the Wild

The Amur Tigress teaches her cubs
how to live in the forest. They play
and learn many things. She is their
teacher and keeps them safe as they
learn about their home.

Bonds That Bind

The love between the Amur Tigress
and her cubs is strong. She teaches
them until they are ready to live on
their own. She makes sure they will
be magnificent tigers when they grow
up.

The Amur Tigress shows us the love
and courage of a mother in the wild.

Challenges Faced by Amur Tigress Moms

The Quest for Sustenance

The Amur Tigress works hard to find enough food for her cubs.
She must be good at hunting because it is difficult to find food.
She is strong and always looks after her babies.

Defenders of the Next Generation

The Amur Tigress protects her cubs from danger. She keeps them safe from other animals and people. She is always careful to keep her babies safe.

The Shadow of Human Influence

Humans can be a big problem for the Amur Tigress. Their homes are getting smaller because of us, and some people hunt them. She must fight against these problems to keep her babies and herself safe.

The Amur Tigress is a very loving mother, fighting for her cubs in a world with many dangers.

Conservation and Threats

A Precarious Balance

People cutting down trees and building things threaten the home of the Amur Tigress. This makes her home smaller and makes it hard for her to live.

The Shadow of Poaching

Some people illegally hunt tigers for their parts. This is an enormous threat to the Amur Tigress and her family. We must fight against this to keep her safe.

The Amur Tigress's world is unique, and we need to help protect it and keep it safe for her and her cubs.

United for the Wild

As we face the challenges of protecting the Amur Tigress, hope shines bright. People are creating safe places for tigers. They are also making better anti-poaching teams and starting new projects to help. Countries are working together. They use laws and agreements like CITES to protect these animals.

We can decide the future of the Amur Tigress and her cubs. By acting to save them, we can make sure the wild stays healthy and full of life.

Cultural Significance and Symbolism

Legends of the Forest

The big forest cat, called the Amur Tigress, is not only living among the trees; she is also a star of many ancient tales. People think of her as a mighty and gentle guardian. In holy places and beautiful artwork, they show her as a fearless and grand symbol.

A Symbol of Majesty

In Asian stories, the Amur Tigress is unique. She shows the beauty of the wild and how important it is to keep nature in balance. She is seen as a protector, keeping away dreadful things.

The Tiger in Our Hearts

The Amur Tigress is important to people everywhere. She teaches us to be brave and to take care of those who need help. She reminds us that we need to look after nature.

Her roar tells us to respect and protect the wild, so the Amur Tigress can inspire people for a long time.

Engaging the Reader

Discovering the Tiger Within

Imagine you are an Amur Tigress in the forest. What would you do? How would you live? You can draw yourself like a tiger or write a story about your adventures.

Conservation Heroes

You can help save wildlife. You can raise money, start a club at school, or tell people about the Amur Tigress. Every little thing you do can help.

Fascinating Tiger Facts

Each tiger's stripes are unique. Tigers can eat a lot at once! Learn more cool things about tigers and tell your friends. Knowing more helps you help them.

The Call of the Wild

Our trip with the Amur Tigress has ended but let us keep caring for our planet's amazing animals. Amur Tigress's story teaches us to learn, share, and act.

Conclusion: A Call to the Wild Heart

Our time learning about the Amur Tigress is over, but we are just helping the wild. This story shows us how important it is to speak up for nature. We still have more exploring to do. Next, we will learn about the snow leopard, a mysterious animal living in the mountains. Their story will teach us more about protecting the wild. Let us keep going. We share these stories to protect tigers and snow leopards. They should live freely and safely. Join us to learn more and help these amazing animals.

Glossary:

- **Amur Tigress:** A big cat with orange fur and black stripes, living in forests.

- **Cubs:** baby tigers learning life skills from their mom.

- **Hunting:** How the Amur Tigress catches food for her family.

- **Solitude:** living alone, which is typical for tigers except for mothers with cubs.

- **Territory:** The forest area, an Amur Tigress calls her own.

- **Poaching:** illegal hunting, a big threat to tigers.

- **Conservation:** efforts to protect tigers and their habitat.

- **Predator:** An animal that hunts other animals, like the Amur Tigress.

- **Carnivore:** An animal that eats mostly meat.

- **Camouflage:** The tiger's stripes help it hide in the forest.

- **Siberia** is a cold region in Russia where some Amur Tigers live.

- **Protection:** keeping tigers safe from harm.

CHAPTER 3: SNOW LEOPARD SOJOURNS: THE SILENT SENTINELS OF THE HIGH MOUNTAINS

Introduction to the Snow Leopard

Ghosts of the Mountains

High up in the tallest mountains of the world lives a unique animal—the snow leopard (Panthera uncia).

They are also called "Ghosts of the Mountains." They live in the cold heights of Central and South Asia and are hard to find. People have al-

ways been amazed by how beautiful and mysterious they are.

Masters of Stealth

Picture an animal with thick, shiny fur
that looks just like the snow around
it. This is the snow leopard. It moves
without making a sound and watches
everything carefully. Snow leopards
are exceptionally good at hiding and
moving around the icy cliffs without
being seen.

Guardians of the High Peaks

Snow leopards have been living in the high mountains for a
long time. People in the mountains believe these cats protect
the peaks. They have warm fur and big paws that help them
survive the cold and wind. Snow leopards are strong, even in
the coldest and toughest places on Earth.

Birth and Early Days

Sheltered Beginnings

Snow leopard moms pick the perfect spot for their babies to be born. They choose places that are hidden and safe, like under a cliff. These spots keep the cubs warm and away from danger. This shows how much the mother cares for her babies.

First Steps into a Snowy World

When snow leopard cubs step on the snow for the first time, it is a big moment. They are curious and careful as they learn about their world. Their mom helps them understand how to live in the snow and mountains.

The Bond of Warmth

As the cubs grow, they learn and play in their cozy den. The mom and cubs make a strong family, and this time is important. It helps the cubs grow up to be strong and ready for life in the mountains.

Raising the Next Generation

Mountain Lessons

In their mountain home, snow leopard cubs learn important things from their mom. She shows them how to jump on rocks and hunt quietly. These lessons are fun but also teach them how to live on their own.

Growth Through Play

Playing with their siblings is not just fun—it helps the cubs get stronger and smarter. They practice jumping, keeping their balance, and using their strength. Playtime is a big part of getting ready for grown-up life.

The Path to Independence

As the cubs get older, they learn to hunt and live by themselves. Their mom has taught them well, and now they can take care of themselves. This is when they start living on their own and keep the snow leopard family going strong in the mountains.

Family Bonds and Social Dynamics

The Maternal Bond

A snow leopard mom and her cubs have a unique connection. The mom works hard to keep her cubs safe and teaches them everything they need to know. She helps them learn how to live alone, which is what snow leopards do. This strong family bond helps the cubs become successful adults.

Path to Solitude

As time goes by, the cubs start to do more on their own. They move away from their mom and the den. This is normal for snow leopards. They grow up to live alone and have their own space in the mountains. The way they move from being with their mom to living alone shows how snow leopards are a loving family. They are also animals that like to be alone.

Lesser-Known Features and Behaviors

Silent Whispers

Snow leopards are the quiet guardians of the mountains. They talk to each other in ways that we cannot hear. Sometimes they growl and purr. But they mostly use smells to mark their space and tell other snow leopards they are there. This unique way of talking helps them stay hidden and move like ghosts in the mountains.

Adaptations to the Cold

Snow leopards are made to live in very cold places high up in the mountains. They have thick fur to keep them warm and big, furry feet that work like snowshoes. They use their long, fluffy tails to keep their faces warm and to balance when they run and jump. These unique features help them live where it is very cold.

Predatory Challenges

It is not easy for snow leopards to find food in the mountains. They must be strong and smart to hunt in places where it is hard to see, and the air is thin. Sometimes they walk a long way to find something to eat. If they do not catch anything, they might get very hungry. But snow leopards are great at living in one of the hardest places on Earth.

The Path to Adulthood

Survivors of the Summit

Baby snow leopards start their life in the beautiful but tough mountains. They must learn many things to become strong adults who can live alone. Their mom helps them learn to play and hunt. Becoming an adult means they have learned to be strong and smart. They are like the mountaintops where they live.

Legacy of the Mountains

Snow leopard moms teach their children everything they know. They show them how to hunt and how to live in the mountains. When the young snow leopards grow up, they leave and start their own families. They use what their moms taught them. This is how snow leopards keep living in the mountains.

A New Cycle Begins

When young snow leopards go out into the towering mountains, they use what they learned when they were little. They find partners and have cubs of their own. This is how the life of snow leopards goes on and on.

Conservation Efforts and Impact

Vanishing Vistas

Snow leopards are in danger because their icy homes are changing due to the Earth getting warmer. People also hunt them for their beautiful fur. Sometimes, they fight with mountain people. They do so because they hunt the same animals. These problems make it hard for snow leopards to survive.

Global Guardianship

People all over the world are working together to help save snow leopards. They are trying to find ways for people and snow leopards to live together safely. They are also working to stop people from hunting snow leopards. These efforts give us hope that snow leopards will keep living in the mountains.

The Legacy of Snow Leopard Mothers

Echoes in the High Peaks

Snow leopard moms are strong and important to the mountains. They work hard to take care of their cubs in the cold, tall mountains. They make sure their babies grow up to keep the snow leopard family going. This helps the whole mountain stay healthy and full of life.

A Call to the Mountains

The story of snow leopard moms and their cubs tells us how important it is to take care of nature. It reminds us to protect these amazing animals and the mountains they live in. By working to save snow leopards, we also help keep our planet beautiful. Let us be inspired by snow leopard moms and work together to make sure these animals are around for a long time.

Engaging with Snow Leopard Sojourns

Interactive Exploration:

Create a mini world where snow leopards live! Build a diorama with tall mountains and rocky places and make a little snow leopard out of felt or clay. Learn about the people who live in the same places as snow leopards in Central and South Asia. This will help you understand how people, animals, and the land are all connected. It will show why we should care about them.

Conservation Advocacy:

Be a voice for snow leopards! Learn about the problems they face. The world is getting warmer, and humans are moving into their space. Tell your friends, family, and neighbors about snow leopards. You can use social media, school projects, or community talks. You can even help raise money for groups that work to protect where snow leopards live. Every little bit helps these mountain ghosts!

Fascinating Facts:

Find out cool things about snow leopards and share them with everyone! Did you know snow leopards can jump six times their body length? That is like you are leaping over a school bus! Also, their thick tails help keep them from falling and keep them warm like a scarf. Knowing these amazing facts makes it even more important to look after snow leopards.

Whispering Legacy: A Tribute to Snow Leopard Mothers

In the big, beautiful mountains, snow leopard moms are strong. They are lovely and take great care of their families. They make sure snow leopards keep living in some of the coldest, hardest places on Earth. They move quietly through the snow. They are important for keeping their home right.

This tribute is about celebrating these snow leopard moms. It also reminds us we need to save them and their wild homes. Their legacy is all about the wild's strong spirit. Let us promise to help nature and wildlife live together in peace.

Glossary

- **Snow Leopard:** A big cat with thick fur, living in the mountains.

- **Cubs:** Young snow leopards that learn from their mother.

- **Alpine:** High mountains where snow leopards live.

- **Camouflage:** How snow leopards' fur helps them blend into the snow.

- **Territory:** The area a snow leopard roams and hunts in.

- **Endangered:** Snow leopards are at risk of disappearing.

- **Predator:** Snow leopards are top hunters in their habitat.

- **Solitary:** Living alone, which is common for snow leopards.

- **Ecosystem:** The community of animals and plants where snow leopards live.

- **Conservation:** Actions to protect snow leopards and their homes.

- **Adaptation:** Special traits that help snow leopards survive in the cold.

- **Stealth:** Moving quietly to surprise their prey.

CHAPTER 4: JAGUAR CHRONICLES: MOTHERS OF THE MIST

Introduction to the Jaguar

Majestic Predators of the Americas

In the lush jungles and wetlands of the Americas, the jaguar is a symbol of wild beauty.

This big cat is the largest in the Americas and has a strong body and beautiful spotted fur. Jaguars can live in many places, from forests to swamps, showing that they are good at adapting. Their presence indicates

a diverse range of plants and animals in the area, as well as a healthy environment.

Masters of Stealth

Jaguars are great at hiding, thanks to their spotted coats that help them blend in. They can sneak up on their prey without being seen. Jaguars are also amazing swimmers, which is rare for big cats. These skills make the jaguar a top predator in its home, where it is both respected and feared.

Solitary and Secretive

Jaguars usually live alone; each having their own large area to hunt and raise their babies. Mother jaguars must hunt and protect their territory while also caring for their cubs. They are particularly good at staying hidden, which helps keep their babies safe in the rainforest.

Birth and Early Life

Selecting the Sanctuary: How Jaguar Mothers Choose the Perfect Den

Jaguar moms pick where to have their babies very carefully. They look for places in the rainforest that are well hidden and close to water. This keeps the baby jaguars safe from other animals and severe weather.

Newborns in the Nest: The crucial first days of a cub's life

When jaguar cubs are born, they need a lot of care. They cannot see and depend on their mom for everything. The first few weeks are important for staying safe and getting stronger. As the cubs grow, they start to learn about the world around them with their mom watching over them.

Steps Toward Discovery: From Dependence to the First Explorations

As jaguar cubs get older, they start to explore more and learn about life in the rainforest. Their mom teaches them what they need to know to survive. The den is like a school where they learn to be strong and smart, just like their mom.

Growth and Development

Nurturing the Hunter Within

Jaguar moms are the best teachers for their little ones. In the deep green of the rainforest, they show their cubs how to live. They teach them to swim through rivers, climb tall trees, and sneak up on prey. Every lesson is about getting ready to live on their own. The mom teaches with care, making sure her cubs know how to manage both land and water.

The Family's Invisible Threads

Even hidden in the leaves, jaguar families are close. They play together, clean each other's fur, and hunt as a team. This is not just about being a family; it is also how cubs learn about the world and their place in it. From these moments, cubs learn to be true jaguars.

From Play to Predation

Growing up means moving from playtime to learning how to hunt. Their mom watches. Cubs practice pouncing and moving quietly. They also practice being strong and graceful, like a jaguar. This time is important because it gets cubs ready to live by themselves later. They are learning how to be the rulers of the rainforest.

Family Bonds and Social Dynamics

Bonds in Solitude

Baby jaguars feel a strong connection to their family, even though they will live alone one day. The time they spend with their mom and siblings shapes how they will act and hunt when they grow up. Learning to work together and compete is key to becoming a good jaguar.

Pathway to Independence

Moms help their cubs grow up by teaching them to hunt, find their way, and mark their space. They do this slowly, waiting until the cubs are ready to be on their own. When cubs finally leave,

it shows that they are ready to face the rainforest by themselves.

Legacy of Learning

As cubs start their own lives, they remember what their family taught them. The skills and lessons they learned early on are important for living alone. Moving from being with family to going solo is a substantial change. It is the start of their own adventure in the big, green world.

Challenges and Threats

Jungle Perils

The rainforest is full of life, but it is also full of dangers for young jaguars. They must watch out for other animals, learn to move through thick trees, and be careful around water. These tough times make them smarter and stronger.

The Human Footprint

Humans are making life hard for jaguars. Cutting down trees, taking over their land, and living too close can hurt jaguar families. We need to keep their homes safe. We do this by making sure there are places where they can live without trouble from people.

A Unified Front for Conservation

To keep jaguars safe, we need to work together. We must protect their homes, study them, and teach everyone about them. We need to make sure jaguars and people can live together without problems. Let us all help to keep these amazing cats around for a long time.

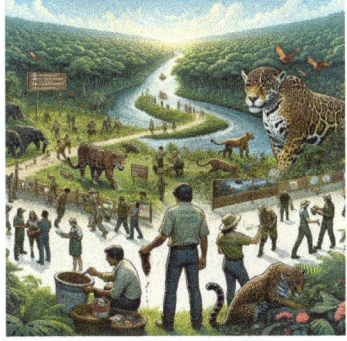

The Path to Adulthood

Embracing Independence

When jaguar cubs grow up, they must start living on their own. This means finding their own place in the jungle and learning to be both the hunter and the protector. This change shows how tough they are and gets them ready for their lives as grown-up jaguars.

Claiming the Wilderness

Young jaguars must find their own space in the jungle. This is their way of making sure they have a place to live and raise their own families. They show they are in charge by leaving their scent around their area. By do-

ing this, they help keep the jungle full of life.

Guardians of the Green

By making their own territories, young jaguars help take care of the rainforest. They keep the number of other animals exactly right, which is good for the whole jungle. This job of looking after their home is something their moms taught them. As they grow up, they keep the spirit of the jaguar alive in the wild green places of the Americas.

Safeguarding the Silent Predator

The jaguar is also known as Panthera onca. It is at risk because its home faces many threats. These threats include being split up, hunted, and taken over by humans. To save this amazing animal, people and groups are working together. They are making rules to stop hunting and creating safe paths for jaguars to walk through their land. This keeps jaguar families strong. It lets them move freely, which is vital for their health.

Apex Architects of the Americas

Jaguars are important for keeping the environment balanced. They are at the top of the food chain, which means they help control the number of other animals. This stops many animals from eating all the plants. It keeps the rainforest and other places healthy. By protecting jaguars, we also care for much land. Many different plants and animals live there.

A Collective Call to Action

The future of jaguars depends on us working together. We need to protect their homes. We need to teach people about them. And we need to ensure they can live with humans safely. We must support projects that help jaguars and make rules to keep their homes safe. Caring for jaguars shows we are doing our part. We are looking after our planet and all its life.

The Legacy of Jaguar Mothers

Guardians of the Future

Jaguar moms are strong and wise, and they work hard to take care of their babies in the rainforest. They teach their cubs how to live and hunt, which is important for keeping jaguars around. These moms are not just taking care of their own cubs; they are making sure the whole species survives.

Lessons from the Wild

The story of jaguar moms and their cubs is unique. It shows us how tough and loving they are, and how all living things are connected. Jaguar moms help keep the rainforest balanced. Their work teaches us about family and caring for our environment.

Engaging with Jaguar Tales

Crafting the Jaguar's World

Artistic Adventures: Get creative with art projects about jaguars and the rainforest. Draw, paint, or make models to show how beautiful and full of life their home is.

Build a small model of the rainforest. Use it to learn about where jaguars live. Add trees, water, and a place for the jaguar to stay hidden.

Becoming a Conservation Advocate

Conservation Projects: Help with or start a project to save jaguars. You could give a talk at school, make a garden that looks like a jaguar's home, or raise money for animals.

Learn about rainforests. Find out about the problems they face. Learn why they are important for jaguars and our planet. Tell other people what you learn.

Jaguar Journey Passport

Passport to the Rainforest: Make a 'Jaguar Journey Passport.' Use it to track what you do and learn about jaguars and their homes. Fill it with stamps for each thing you discover or help with.

Virtual Safaris and Real-World Actions

Take a Virtual Jaguar Safari. Watch online videos or documentaries to see jaguars in their natural home. Write down interesting facts and think about how you can help them even from far away.

Adopt a Jaguar: You can help save jaguars by 'adopting' one through a wildlife group. Your support can help with research and keeping jaguars safe in the wild.

Conclusion: Guardianship Echoes: Honoring the Jaguar Legacy

Rainforest Sentinels

Jaguar moms are not just hunters; they are protectors of the rainforest. They show their cubs how to live in their beautiful, watery home. They are crucial for keeping the jungle balanced and healthy.

A Legacy of Wisdom

Jaguar moms teach their cubs how to survive and how to take care of the environment. This helps make sure jaguars will live in the rainforest for a long time.

Coexistence and Conservation

We have an important job to do to keep jaguars safe. We need to make sure they have places to live and learn how to live with them without causing problems. Taking care of jaguars means we are also taking care of the rainforest.

Inspiring Action

The story of the jaguar mom is a reminder that we need to help protect these amazing cats. We should support projects that save them. They also teach others about why it is important to keep our planet's animals and plants safe.

Glossary:

- **Jaguar:** A large cat with spotted fur, living in the Americas.

- **Cubs:** Baby jaguars who depend on their mom for food and protection.

- **Rainforest:** A dense, green forest where it rains a lot, home to jaguars.

- **Camouflage:** The jaguar's spots help it hide while hunting.

- **Territory:** The area where a jaguar lives and hunts.

- **Predator:** Jaguars are animals that hunt other animals for food.

- **Conservation:** Working to protect jaguars and their homes.

- **Adaptation:** Special skills jaguars must live in different environments.

- **Stealth:** Moving silently to catch prey unexpectedly.

- **Solitary:** Jaguars usually live and hunt alone.

- **Endangered:** Jaguars are at risk because of habitat loss and hunting.

- **Ecosystem:** The community of living things in the rainforest.

Chapter 5: Swift Shadows: The Journey of a Cheetah Mother

Introduction to the Species

The cheetah (Acinonyx Jubatus) races through life on the wide-open African savannas.

It also runs in the hidden grasslands of Iran. Known as the quickest animal on land, the cheetah is a living example of how nature can adapt and survive.

Physical Characteristics

The cheetah's body is perfectly designed for speed. It has a slim shape, long, and strong legs, and a coat of golden yellow with black spots that help it hide in tall grasses. Its light bones and big nose help it breathe fast, letting it run up to seventy miles per hour!

Habitat

Cheetahs love wide, flat spaces. They can see far and run fast in places like the African savannas and grasslands. They need these open areas to hunt and to watch out for other animals. Iran also has some cheetahs. They live in various places. This shows how well they can adapt.

Behavior and Diet

Cheetahs hunt in the daytime, using their amazing eyesight to find food far away. They sneak up on their prey, then sprint super-fast to catch it by surprise. They usually eat smaller animals like gazelles. Cheetahs must be smart about hunting. They must eat quickly because bigger animals might steal their food.

Birth and Early Life

Birthing Practices

A mother cheetah picks a very hidden place to have her babies, to keep them safe from other animals. She carefully chooses a spot that is private and safe.

The cheetah mom has her cubs quietly, with three to five in a litter. They are born tiny and cannot see yet. The mom must watch them all the time to keep them safe.

Cub Development

Baby cheetahs have a unique hair that helps them blend in with the grass. The mother cheetah hunts just long enough to feed herself and stays close to her cubs to protect them. As the cubs grow and start to see and move, they stick close to their mom. She teaches them all they need to know to live in the wild.

Growth and Development

Mother's Hunting Strategies with Young Cubs

When she has cubs, the mother cheetah must hunt in a smart way. She chooses where to keep her cubs very carefully and hunts fast so she can get back to them quickly.

Cub Vulnerability

When the mom is hunting, the cubs are in danger of being hurt by other animals. The mom moves her cubs to new hiding spots often and comes back to them as soon as she can after hunting.

Learning to Hunt

The cubs watch their mom and play with each other to learn how to hunt. As they grow up, they get stronger and start to hunt on their own. They go from depending on their mom to being independent.

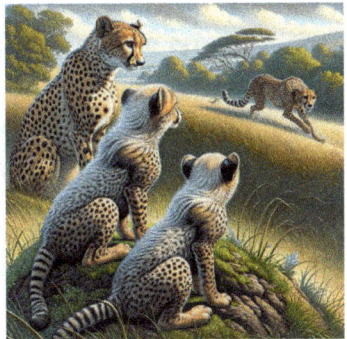

Bonding and Social Learning

Sibling Play

Cubs learn a lot by playing with their brothers and sisters. They practice chasing and catching each other, which helps them learn how to hunt for real when they grow up.

Mother's Role

The mother cheetah is the main teacher for her cubs. She shows them how to hunt and live with other cheetahs. She teaches them how to communicate and what to do in the cheetah world.

Challenges and Threats

Predation and Competition

Cheetah mothers and their cubs face many dangers. They must watch out for other big animals like lions, hyenas, and leopards. These predators can hurt the cubs or take the cheetahs' food. Cheetahs must be fast and smart to stay away from these dangers. The mom must always be on alert to keep her cubs fed and safe.

Human Impact

People also cause problems for cheetahs. Their homes are getting smaller because of farms and cities growing. Sometimes farmers kill cheetahs to protect their animals. People sometimes catch cheetah cubs to sell as pets. These things make it even harder for cheetahs to survive.

Journey to Independence

Path to Solitude

Cheetah cubs must learn to live by themselves. They watch their mom and practice until they can hunt. The mom decides when to let them try on their own. Each time they do not catch something, they learn to be better hunters. Eventually, when they are about 1.5 to 2 years old, they leave their mom and start their own lives.

Conservation and the Species' Future

Conservation Status

Cheetahs are in trouble and need our help. Their homes are being destroyed. People are killing them and taking their babies. To save them, people are trying to fix their homes, stop poaching, and help people and cheetahs get along.

Role in the Ecosystem

Cheetahs are important. They control the number of other animals. This keeps the grasslands healthy. If we lose cheetahs, the whole place where they live could change, which would be bad for lots of plants and animals.

Reflections on Mother's Care

Crucial Maternal Role

Cheetah moms have a big job. They keep their cubs safe, teach them to hunt, and help them understand how to be a cheetah. What they do is important for their babies and the future of all cheetahs.

Broader Implications

The story of cheetah moms is about more than just cheetahs. It shows how all moms in nature work hard to take care of their babies. This helps keep all kinds of animals around and keeps the world balanced.

In the Cheetah's Footsteps: Activities for Young Conservationists

Interactive Exploration and Conservation Engagement

You can learn about cheetahs and help save them with fun projects. Write stories, make art, and tell others about why we need to protect cheetahs.

Creative Activities

A Day in the Life: Write a story about what it is like to be a cheetah cub for a day. Talk about what you see, do, and learn.

Savannah Scenes: Draw or paint a picture of cheetahs in the wild. Show how beautiful they and their home are.

Cheetah Diaries: Pretend you are a cheetah mom or cub and write about your day. This can help you understand what life is like for them.

Conservation in Action

Protecting the Fastest Cats: Find out about groups that help cheetahs. Then, share what you learn with others.

Voices for Cheetahs: Write letters to tell people how important it is to save cheetahs. Your words can help make a difference.

Art for Advocacy: Make a poster to show why we should save cheetahs. Put it up at school or online to get people to care.

Discover More

There will be a list of good places to learn more about cheetahs and other big cats. This will include websites, groups, and movies. They tell you more about these amazing animals.

By doing these projects, we can all help make sure cheetahs keep running free for a long time. Let us use our creativity and passion to protect them.

Conclusion: Sprinting Towards Hope: The Cheetah Mother's Legacy

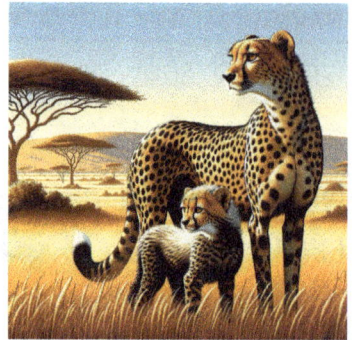

There is a deep lesson in the cheetah mother's quick journey: being strong in the face of hardship. No one else's story is as important as hers. As guardians of the Earth, we all live on, we need to change things. We have a choice to make. It could endanger these beautiful animals and their wild homes or protect them.

Let us take on the cheetah's spirit: quick, agile, and strong. We can all work together to protect the wild's heritage. We can ensure that the cheetah sprints across the savannah to stay alive. This lets them live on for future generations. Together, we are strong, and when we act, we find hope. Let us be a shining example of protection. Let us protect the beauty of biodiversity and the hope for a peaceful future.

Glossary:

- **Cheetah:** The fastest land animal, known for its speed.

- **Cubs:** Young cheetahs learning to survive from their mom.

- **Savanna:** Grassy plains in Africa, a home to many cheetahs.

- **Camouflage:** Cheetah's spotted coat helps it blend in with the grass.

- **Predator:** Cheetahs hunt other animals for food.

- **Solitary:** Adult cheetahs mostly live and hunt alone.

- **Vulnerable:** Cheetahs face dangers from larger animals and humans.

- **Endangered:** The cheetah population in the wild is critically low.

- **Habitat:** The natural home or environment of an animal.

Chapter 6: Silent Shadows: The Journey of a Cougar Mother

Welcome to the World of Cougars!

Majestic Cats:

Let us take a walk into the world of the cougar (Puma Concolor), a wildcat that is exceptionally good at hiding and moves with beauty.

These big cats have fur that helps them blend in with where they live. They live in snowy Canada and green forests in South America. Cougars glide and move silently. They show

they can live in many places and are powerful hunters.

Cougars Alone:

Cougars like to live by themselves. They have learned to do this over a long time. They travel a lot to find food, using their sharp senses and quiet moves. Cougars hunt animals like deer and small creatures. They are important because they help keep things balanced, but people do not see them often. They are like quiet shadows in the wild.

This is just the beginning of learning about cougars. We will look more at how they live alone, how they hunt, and how they take care of their babies. The life of a cougar mom is a story of being tough, caring, and making it on her own.

Baby Cougars and Their First Days

Secret Homes for Babies:

Cougar moms pick hidden spots in the wild to have their babies. These secret homes can be in thick bushes or under rocks. They choose these spots to keep their little ones safe from danger. This shows how much a cougar mom wants to protect her babies when they are most at risk.

Baby Cougars' First Adventures:

Cougar babies are born in these quiet homes. They cannot see and need their mom a lot when they first come into the world. The mom keeps them warm, feeds them, and watches over them. When the babies see and walk, they learn about life. The time they spend with their mom is important. It gets them ready for the bigger world outside.

Growing Up:

The baby cougars get bigger and learn more with their mom's help. They learn about living in the wild and what they need to do to survive. This time is about growing up, playing, and learning. What their mom teaches them will help them become strong cougars in the future.

Getting Bigger and Learning to Hunt

Learning to Catch Food:

Cougars are quiet when they hunt. Moms teach their babies how to hunt by showing them how to sneak up on food and catch it at the right time. It is important for the babies to learn this so they can live on their own later. They need to be able to catch their own food to survive.

From Playing to Hunting:

As baby cougars get bigger, their play fights become a real practice for living in the wild. They learn to move in their home, catch food, and sneak up on it. This time is about changing from needing their mom to being able to live on their own.

Becoming Independent:

When cougars grow from kids to adults, they do things by themselves. They try hunting alone, get better at it, and start to spend less time with their mom. This change is important. It makes sure they can live alone in the wild, just like other cougars do.

Family Life and Getting Along

Siblings:

Cougar babies learn about life by being with their brothers and sisters. They sometimes fight and play, but they also take care of each other. This helps them learn about living alone and being part of the wild.

Growing Up Strong:

As the babies grow, their mom shows them how to take care of themselves. She teaches them how to find food and make their way in the big wild world. This is a key time for them. It helps them move from being young and needing help to being grown up and on their own.

Lessons for Life:

The things cougar babies learn when they are young stay with them as they grow. They learn how to hunt, where to live, and how to be part of nature. These lessons come from the strong bond between the mom and her babies. They help the next cougars to live well in the wild and keep the cougar family going strong.

Fascinating Cougar Facts

The Secret Sounds of Cougars

Even though cougars are big and strong, they do not roar like lions. Instead, they talk to each other with quiet sounds. These include purring, hissing, growling, and whistling. These soft noises help cougars talk to their babies and other cougars. They do so without making much noise. Too much noise might scare away their food or attract danger.

Cougars' Unique Signs

Cougars leave little clues in their home area to tell other cougars, "This is my space." They scratch trees and leave scents that are like secret messages to other animals. This way, they can live alone. They will not have too many arguments with other cougars.

Cougars Can Leap High

Cougars have an amazing ability to jump. They can jump up to twenty feet straight up from standing still and leap as far as forty feet across. This helps them surprise their prey and move around their homes very well.

Cougars' Coats Help Them Hide

A cougar's fur helps it blend in with the trees and ground. This unique coat changes with the seasons and in various places so that they can always hide well. This helps them sneak up on their food and stay safe.

Cougars Grow Up to Live Alone

Cougars learn to live by themselves when they grow up. Their moms teach them how to hunt and mark their area. This helps them get ready to have their own space in the wild.

Young Cougars Look for New Homes

When they are ready, young cougars leave their birthplace to find their own place. This is a big adventure with many new things to learn, like finding food and staying away from other animals.

Cougars Learn Important Lessons from Their Moms

The things that cougar moms teach their babies are important. These lessons help them survive on their own and keep them safe as they grow up.

Cougars Face Some Big Problems

Cougars must deal with dangers in the wild, like other animals, and changes made by people. It is important to help them by keeping their homes safe and not taking away too much of their space.

People Can Affect Cougars a Lot

When people build homes and roads in the wild, it can make life hard for cougars. We need to find ways to live together without hurting their homes or food.

We Need to Help Cougars

Cougars are a big part of keeping nature healthy. We should work hard to protect them and the places where they live. By doing this, we help many other animals and plants too.

Fun Cougar Activities

Make a Cougar Den

Activity: Build a model of a cougar den using things like cardboard and blankets. Think about how cougars stay safe and hidden in their dens.

Pretend to Be a Cougar

Activity: Write a story or draw a comic about being a cougar cub exploring your home. What adventures do you have? How do you solve problems?

Learn and Teach About Cougars

Make a poster or presentation about cougars. Include their homes and why they are important. Share what you learn with others to help cougars.

Help Cougars in Your Community

Activity: Set up a day to teach people about cougars and how we can protect them. You can play games and share fun facts about these animals.

Discover Cougar Facts

Activity: Find out cool facts about cougars and tell your friends and family. Share ways we can all help save cougars.

Create Cougar Art

Activity: Draw or paint pictures of cougars or use an app to make cougar art. Show your art to others to get them interested in helping cougars.

These activities can help you learn more about cougars and what we can do to take care of them and their homes.

Conclusion: Cougars are Quiet, Caring Protectors

Cougars live in the wild with strength and kindness. The mom cougar shows us how to be careful and loving. She is a silent protector of her babies and teaches them how to survive.

You Can Help Cougars Too

The story of the cougar teaches us we all share the wild and need to look after it. It asks you to care for the wild, speak up for animals like cougars, and make sure they have a safe place to live for a long time.

Glossary:

- **Cougar:** A large, solitary cat that lives in North and South America.

- **Cubs:** Baby cougars that stay with their mom until they can survive alone.

- **Territory:** The large area where a cougar hunts and lives.

- **Predator:** Cougars are animals that eat other animals to live.

- **Camouflage:** Cougars have fur that helps them blend into their surroundings.

- **Conservation:** Protecting cougars and their natural habitats.

- **Solitary:** Cougars usually live and hunt by themselves.

- **Stealth:** Moving quietly and unseen to approach prey.

- **Habitat:** The type of environment where cougars live, like forests and mountains.

- **Endangered:** Cougars face threats from habitat loss and conflict with humans.

- **Adaptation:** Special traits that help cougars survive in various environments.

- **Ecosystem:** The community of animals and plants that interact with cougars in their habitat.

Chapter 7 - Lynx Chronicles: The Enigmatic World of Eurasian Lynx Mothers

Meet the Eurasian Lynx

Mysterious Cats of the Forest

Deep in the forests of Europe and Asia, there is a cat called the Eurasian Lynx that moves so quietly, it is like a ghost.

Its fur helps it hide among the trees and leaves. This shy animal has sharp eyes for spotting things in the forest and walks so softly that it

hardly makes a sound. The lynx is a secret part
of the wild places it lives in.

Lynxes Love Big Spaces

The Eurasian Lynx likes to have
a lot of room and lives in huge
forests from Europe all the way
to cold Siberia. These cats are
great at sneaking up on the animals they hunt, even when it
is snowy, or the bushes are very thick. They have their own
unique forest areas. They keep to themselves and know every
part well.

Moms Are Very Caring

Even though lynxes usually like to
be alone. Mother lynxes are very
loving and care for their babies.
These moms show their little ones
how to live in the wild and hunt
for food. They are incredibly quiet. But they are always there for
their cubs. They teach them all
they need to know to grow up strong and smart.

Our journey to learn about the Eurasian Lynx starts with understanding them. They are amazing animals. They lead quiet

lives. As we follow their tracks in the snow, we will learn more about how they live and stay hidden. We will also learn about the unique bond between a lynx mom and her cubs.

Cubs' First Days

Cozy Hidden Homes

In the peaceful forests where the Eurasian Lynx lives, mother lynxes have a vital job. They must find the perfect place for their babies to be born. They pick spots where it is quiet and safe, like thick bushes or caves. These places are unique. They are where the lynx cubs start their lives. They are safe from danger and cozy in the quiet forest.

Welcome to the World, Little Lynxes

When lynx cubs are born, they are small and cannot see yet. They depend on their mom to keep them warm and feed them. The first few weeks are crucial. This is when the cubs start to grow and learn about the world from their safe home.

Stepping Out into the Forest

As the cubs get a little bigger, they begin to explore outside their home. They follow their mom and learn about all the sights and sounds of the forest. These first adventures are vital. They help the cubs learn to live in the wild as adults.

The story of the Eurasian Lynx cubs is all about how they grow up in the forest with their mom's help. It is a story about learning to survive. It starts in the secret places where they are born and goes to their first steps into the big world. The world is the beautiful forests they call home.

Growing Up

Learning to Hunt

Mother lynxes teach their cubs how to hunt in the quiet forest. They show them how to move without making noise and how to wait for the best moment to catch their food. These lessons are important because they help the cubs learn to get food on their own when they are older.

Staying Warm in the Cold

The forest where the lynxes live can get very cold in the winter. But lynx cubs are born ready for the cold. They have thick fur to keep them warm. They have big paws that work like snowshoes. They learn from their mom how to find shelter and stay warm. These unique things about them help them do well even when it is freezing outside.

As they grow, lynx cubs learn everything they need to live in the big forest. Their mom teaches them to hunt and stay warm. They have unique things to help them live in the cold. They learn to be strong and smart, like the Eurasian Lynx should be. They continue the story of their kind in the snowy forests.

Eurasian Lynx Families: Life in the Wild

Fun and Learning: Lynx Cubs with Their Siblings

The lynx cubs live in quiet forests. They learn about life with their siblings. They play together, which might look like just fun, but it is also important. When they play, they are practicing for when they must live on their own. They learn about hunting, hiding, and being careful, which are all things they need to know to survive.

A Mother's Teaching: From Cubs to Grown-ups

As the lynx cubs get older, their mom starts teaching them how to be independent. She shows them how to hunt quietly and carefully in the snow. This time with their mom helps them get ready to live by themselves in the wild forest.

This is a lynx's life. They play with siblings and learn from their mom. It is all about getting ready to live alone. It is important. It helps them become strong and smart. Then, they can manage living in the forest alone.

Overcoming the Cold: Lynx in Winter

Eurasian lynxes are good at living in cold places. They have big, furry paws that let them walk on top of the snow without sinking. Their thick fur keeps them warm, and they know how to hunt and stay safe in the snow. These unique skills help them do well as hunters in their snowy world.

Humans and Lynxes: Finding a Way to Live Together

Sometimes, the places where lynxes live get changed by people who build things or cut down trees. This can make it hard for lynxes to find food and a safe place to live. People who care about animals are trying to find ways to help lynxes. They want to ensure there are paths for lynxes to walk safely. They also want to teach people to live without hurting lynx homes.

Talking about these problems is important. It helps us see how we can live with lynxes and keep the forests healthy for all animals.

Growing Up and Going Solo

Becoming Independent

When lynx cubs grow up, they learn to do everything by themselves. They explore, mark their own area, and hunt. This is how they become adults and start to live alone in the big forest.

Finding a Mate

Grown-up lynxes usually live alone, but when it is time to have cubs, they look for a partner. They have a unique way of calling to find each other. This is how they keep making sure there are more lynxes in the forest.

The story of a lynx growing up is about learning to live alone and then finding a mate to start their own family. This is how they make sure there will always be lynxes in the forest.

Helping Lynxes Stay Safe

Protecting the Quiet Hunters

Eurasian lynxes need our help. Their homes are getting smaller and there's not always enough food. Some people are working to protect lynxes. They keep their homes safe and make sure there are enough animals for them to hunt.

Keeping the Forest Healthy

Lynxes are important because they help keep the number of other animals balanced. This is good for the whole forest. By helping lynxes, we also help the forest and all the other animals that live there.

Learning From Lynx Moms

Mothers Know Best

Lynx moms are great at taking care of their cubs in the cold forests. They choose the best places for their cubs to be born and teach them how to live in the wild. This helps the cubs grow up to be good hunters and live on their own.

Lessons From the Wild

The way lynx moms look after their cubs teaches us about being strong and caring. These lessons are not just for animals but for everyone. They show us how important it is to help each other and grow up to be the best we can be.

The story of lynx moms and their cubs shows us how all moms in nature work hard. They take care of their young and teach them about life.

Discover the World of Eurasian Lynxes

Make a Mini Lynx Forest

Activity: Use a box, cotton balls, and sticks to create a snowy forest where a lynx might live. Add a toy lynx or a picture of one to make your forest feel like a real lynx home.

Pretend to Be a Lynx Cub

Activity: Write a story about a day in the life of a lynx cub. Think about what you would do in the forest. Would you hunt for food or play in the snow? Share your story with others or act it out.

Be a Friend to Lynxes

Activity: Learn all about lynxes and make a project to show others. You can make a poster or a slideshow about where lynxes live, what they eat, and why it is important to keep them safe. Share your project to help everyone learn about lynxes.

Fun With Lynx Facts

Activity: Find out cool things about lynxes, like how they can live in the cold and what makes their paws so unique. Then, assess your friends and family with a quiz to see who knows the most about lynxes.

Write to Help Lynxes

Activity: Write a letter to people who can make a difference for lynxes. Tell them why you care about lynxes and ask how you can help protect them.

Create Lynx Art

Activity: Draw or paint a picture of a lynx or make a digital art-work. Try to show how beautiful lynxes are or imagine them in their forest home. Show your art to others to get them excited about helping lynxes.

These fun activities can help you learn more about Eurasian lynxes. They show why it is important to take care of the lynx's homes. By doing these activities, you can help make sure lynxes have a safe place to live.

A Special Thank You to Lynx Moms

Lynx moms are amazing. They teach their cubs everything about living in the forest and make sure they are safe. They help their cubs grow up to be strong and ready for the wild.

Let Us Learn from Lynxes

Lynx moms and their cubs show us how to take care of each other and the world around us. Their story teaches us to be kind, strong, and smart. It reminds us that it is important to look after our planet and all the animals that live with us.

The story of the lynx is a story about family, growing up, and living in the wild. It is also a story about us and how we can help keep the wild places safe for animals like the lynx.

Glossary:

- **Eurasian Lynx:** A large cat with tufted ears, living in Europe and Asia.

- **Cubs:** Young lynx that learn essential survival skills from their mom.

- **Forest:** The main home of lynx, full of trees and under-brush.

- **Camouflage:** Lynx fur helps them hide while stalking prey.

- **Territory:** The area a lynx patrols and hunts within.

- **Predator:** Lynxes hunt smaller animals for food.

- **Conservation:** Efforts to protect lynxes and their forest homes.

- **Solitary:** Lynxes mostly live alone, except for mothers with cubs.

- **Stealth:** Lynxes hunt by sneaking up on their prey quietly.

- **Endangered:** Some lynx populations are at risk due to habitat loss.

- **Adaptation:** Lynxes have thick fur and strong paws for living in cold forests.

- **Hunting:** The way lynxes catch their food using sharp senses and patience.

Part II

Caracal, Ocelot, Serval, African Golden Cat, Asian Golden Cat, Pallas's Cat, and Fishing Cat

CHAPTER 8- CARACAL CHRONICLES: THE GRACEFUL MOTHERS OF THE SAVANNAH

Introduction to the Caracal

Graceful Hunters:

C aracals are beautiful wild cats that live in the wide-open lands of Africa and Asia.

They are very graceful, moving smoothly and quickly. They have lovely golden-brown fur and are not too big or too small. These cats are great at living in various places and are good at catching their food.

Amazing Ears:

Caracals have something unique about them: their long, black ear tufts. These are not just for looks. They help caracals show feelings and look even more mysterious in the wild. When they have babies, these ear tufts are important for talking to their little ones.

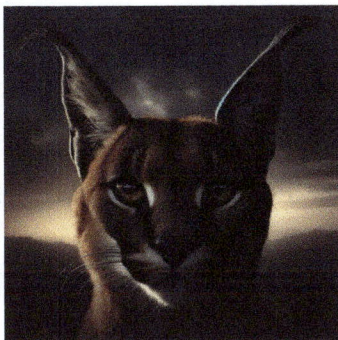

Symbols of Nature:

These cats represent wild nature. They are important for keeping nature balanced and healthy. Caracals like to be alone and are very private animals. They remind us that we need to take care of nature, so it stays beautiful for a long time. We are starting to learn more about caracals. We are learning about how they are as mothers in their natural homes.

Caracal Cubs: A Journey Begins

Safe Birthing Places:

Mother caracals pick very secret spots to have their babies. These places are safe from other animals that might harm the newborn cubs. The spot might be hidden by plants or rocks, and it helps keep the little ones safe.

Loving Care:

Baby caracals are born in a warm and safe place with their mom taking diligent care of them. She keeps them warm, feeds them, and cleans them with licks. This also makes the bond between them strong. When the cubs open their eyes for the first time, their mom is there to protect and teach them.

Teaching to Hunt:

Mother caracals teach their cubs how to hunt without making noise. They do this when the sun is coming up or going down. The mom shows how to move quietly and catch food in a smart way. The cubs learn to be patient and quick.

Growing Up Strong:

As the cubs get older, they start to look and act more like adult caracals. They learn to use their sharp senses, strong legs, and quick jumps to hunt. Playing with their mom and siblings helps them get ready for life on their own.

This part tells us about how caracal cubs grow up and learn to live by themselves, with their mom's help.

Caracal Families and Living Alone

Life Alone:

Caracals mostly live by themselves. They learn early that they will spend a lot of time alone, except when they are young and with their family. Even when they are with their siblings, they are getting ready for the day they will go off on their own.

Growing Up:

The mom caracal teaches her cubs to hunt and to be careful when they are alone. As the cubs get bigger, she lets them try things by themselves. They learn from their mistakes. When they are ready, she sends them off to live their own lives as adult caracals.

We learn here that caracals live mostly alone. But, when they are young, they form strong family bonds. These bonds help them get ready for the future.

Unique Skills and Quiet Talks

Jumping High:

Caracals are amazing because they can jump remarkably high to catch birds flying in the sky. They use their strong back legs to do this.

Night Hunters:

Caracals are active at night. They have great eyesight in the dark, which helps them find and catch their food without being seen.

Quiet Signals:

Caracals also have a quiet way of talking to each other. They use soft sounds, smells, and body movements to send messages. This is how they find mates and tell other caracals about their space.

By learning about these things, we see that caracals are not simply good hunters. They also have interesting ways of living and talking to each other in the wild.

The Path to Adulthood

Journey into Independence:

As caracal kittens grow up, they start to explore the world without their mom's constant care. This is a substantial change for them. They are learning to be alone and take care of themselves. They practice all their mother taught them about living in the wild. They do this until they are ready to have their own space.

Legacy of the Savannah:

Becoming an adult caracal is more than just getting bigger. It is about carrying on with what their mother taught them. They learn to live well in the wild and to keep doing what caracals have always done. This keeps their kind strong. It helps them keep being amazing animals in the wide, open lands they live in.

Here we see how young caracals become adults and start to live alone. They use all the lessons their mothers gave them.

Conservation Efforts and Impact

A Quest for Survival:

Caracals are facing tough times. Their homes are disappearing, and they sometimes have trouble with people. But people who care about animals are working hard to save them. They are fixing up the places where caracals live and stopping people from hurting them. We need to help caracals so they can keep living in the wild.

Guardians of the Balance:

Caracals are important for keeping nature balanced. They help control the number of other animals and keep the land full of various kinds of life. Keeping caracals safe is important not just for them, but for all the plants and animals where they live. This part talks about how caracals keep nature healthy. We need to help them to keep nature working right.

This part tells us how important it is to protect caracals and the places they live in. We need to work together to make sure they stay safe.

The Legacy of Caracal Mothers

Maternal Mastery:

In the dry lands where caracals live, the love between a mother and her babies is the first big lesson in how to survive. The mother caracal teaches her kittens what they need to know to live on their own. She shows them how to hunt, stay safe, and be strong. This part is about how important mother

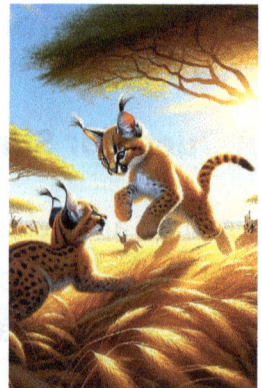

caracals are for their babies and for all caracals.

Echoes of the Wild:

The story of caracal mothers is immensely powerful. It shows us how strong a mother's love is in the wild. They are beautiful and smart, and they know how to manage the tough life they live. This helps us understand how all mothers in nature take care of their babies.

This part talks about how mother caracals teach their kittens. It explains what that means for their future and for nature.

Engaging with Caracal Chronicles

Creative Discoveries:

Learn about caracals by making fun projects. Build a model of a caracal's home or write a story about what a day is like for a caracal kitten. These projects help you be creative and learn more about how caracals live.

Voices for Conservation:

Help caracals by learning about how to protect them. You could do a school project to tell people about caracals. Or, you could collect money to give to animal protection groups. Writing to people who can have influence and telling them to take care of caracals can also help. You can do a lot to keep caracals safe.

Curiosity Unleashed:

Discover cool things about caracals. They can jump extremely high to catch birds in the air. And, they hunt quietly. Share what you learn with others. Do it through talks, pictures, or online. This will help everyone know about these amazing cats. Learning and sharing facts about caracals can make people want to help them.

This part invites you to get involved and help caracals. By doing projects and helping others learn, you can make a significant difference. Also, by talking about caracals, you can help the cats and their homes.

Conclusion: Safeguarding Grace: A Tribute to Caracal Mothers

They live in the wide, open savannah. Life's big dance happens under the big sky. Caracal mothers are the picture of beauty and toughness. They teach their babies how to live and survive. Their love and strength show the spirit of the wild. It is a story about how mothers care for their babies, are strong, and know so much.

This chapter is about celebrating caracal moms and reminding us to take care of nature. Their story is part of nature, and we need to help keep it going. By helping save caracals and their homes, we make sure they and many other animals can keep living.

Let us be inspired by caracals to do our best in taking care of our planet and all its animals. That way, we can keep the beauty and wonder of the wild alive for a long time.

Glossary:

- **Caracal:** A medium-sized wild cat known for its distinctive long ear tufts.

- **Kittens:** Baby caracals who depend on their mother for care and protection.

- **Savannah:** Grassy plains where caracals often live, hunting for birds and rodents.

- **Ear Tufts:** Long fur on the tips of a caracal's ears, helping with communication.

- **Stealth:** The silent way caracals approach their prey.

- **Predator:** Caracals are animals that catch and eat other animals.

- **Conservation:** Working to keep caracals safe in their natural habitats.

- **Solitary:** Caracals usually live and hunt on their own.

- **Adaptation:** Special abilities caracals have to live in different environments.

- **Hunting:** How caracals catch their food using surprise and speed.

- **Territory:** The area a caracal calls its home and defends.

- **Ecosystem:** All the living things in an area and how they interact, including caracals.

Chapter 9: Ocelot Chronicles: The Bond of a Cat Mother

Introduction to the Ocelot

Graceful Hunters:

In the forests that stretch across the Americas, ocelots move with silent steps.

Their fur is a beautiful pattern of spots and stripes, perfect for nighttime hunting.

Home Everywhere:

Ocelots exist in many places, from dense jungles to dry areas with only a few trees. They show us how well they can adjust to different environments, making any place a home.

Mother's Care:

Ocelot stories often tell of the unique bond between mother and cub. Mothers teach their cubs everything they need to know to survive in the wild. Let us start our journey by seeing how ocelot moms are amazing at taking care of and teaching their little ones.

Birth and Early Days

Hidden Birthing Havens:

Ocelot moms pick the best spots in nature to have their babies—places that are quiet and well-hidden. These safe spots protect the little ones from danger and let them take their first breaths in peace. This is the start of a mom's careful watch over her cubs.

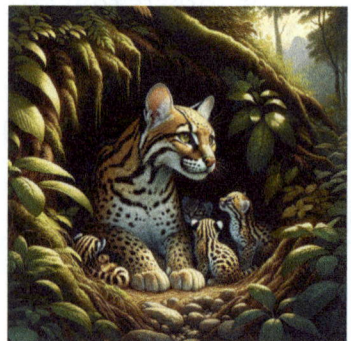

First Steps:

For a baby ocelot, the world is small but full of amazing things. With their mom close by, these little ones with spots start their adventure. They begin to explore, staying close to the safety of their den. Their mom's love helps them grow. She feeds them, keeps them clean, and holds them close, teaching them about life all around them. This time is important because it builds trust and learning for the future.

Raising the Next Generation

Survival Lessons:

In the shadows of the trees, ocelot moms teach their cubs how to stay alive. They show them how to stay hidden and move without being seen. The cubs start learning to hunt with small, simple catches. This play time is really teaching them life-saving skills.

Towards Independence:

As time goes by, the young ocelots start to do things on their own. They get braver and go farther, while their mom watches over them. She helps them when they make mistakes but lets them try things for themselves. This time ends when the young ocelots leave to find their own

places to live, using all they learned from their mom.

Family Bonds and Social Dynamics

The Strength of Sibling Bonds:

They learn and grow stronger together in the light that filters through the trees. They are ocelot brothers and sisters. Playing is more than just fun—it helps them learn how to hunt and understand their world. The siblings' connection is their first lesson. It is in balancing competition and caring.

Solitary yet Connected:

Even though ocelots will live alone when they grow up, the bond with their mom is deep. They learn how to be close and then how to leave and live on their own. The mom's love and teaching are what keep the cubs alive and ready for the future. This part shows us how family ties in the wild are complex but important.

Surviving Challenges

Dangers in the Wild:

Ocelot families face many dangers, from hidden predators to tough weather. Moms are key in keeping their cubs safe, using their instincts and smarts to stay away from danger. This carefulness shows just how hard life can be in the wild.

Human Footprint:

Humans affect the ocelots' home in big ways. Cities growing, trees being cut down, and roads cutting through the land are all big problems. Working to save ocelots and their homes is crucial. It keeps everything balanced. This part tells us about the problems of living together. It explains why we need to protect these pretty cats and their homes.

The Path to Adulthood

Embracing Solitude:

As they grow, ocelot kittens leave their mother's side. This step is important as they learn to live by themselves in the wild. This change is part of becoming an adult ocelot and getting ready for life alone.

Legacy of Learning:

An ocelot mother teaches her kittens many things. They learn how to hunt, stay hidden, and be smart in the wild. These lessons help them when they grow up. The kittens use what their mother taught them to live well and keep their kind going.

Conservation Efforts and Impact

A Species at Risk:

Ocelots are beautiful and mysterious, but they are in danger. Their homes are being destroyed, and sometimes people hunt them. They need our help to stay safe and keep living in the wild.

Global and Local Efforts:

People are working hard to save ocelots. They make laws to protect them and try to keep their homes safe. Scientists study ocelots to learn how to help them. Everyone can help, from local people to friends around the world. Working together, we can make sure ocelots stay a part of the wild.

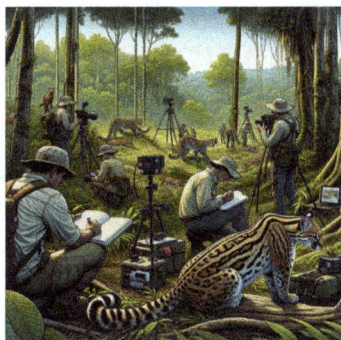

The Legacy of Ocelot Mothers

Influence Beyond Survival:

Ocelot mothers do a lot for their kittens. They teach them how to live and be safe. This love and teaching are important for the kittens' future. This part is about how a mother's care helps her kittens grow up to be strong ocelots.

Echoes in Ecosystems:

Ocelot mothers help more than just their own kittens. They keep nature healthy and full of life. This story shows us why saving ocelots is good for the entire world. They help keep everything in nature working together.

Engaging with Ocelot Tales

Dive Into the Ocelot's World:

Make an Ocelot Home: Build a model of where ocelots live using things from around your house. Add trees, a den, and animals they might hunt. This helps you learn about ocelot homes.

Play as an Ocelot: Pretend you are an ocelot for a day. What would you do? This game helps you understand what life is like for an ocelot.

Be an Ocelot Advocate:

Make a Club for Ocelots: Start a group with friends who care about animals. You can all learn about ocelots and help them together.

Speak Up for Ocelots: Write to people who can be effective, like animal groups or the government. Tell them we need to save ocelots and their homes.

Discover and Share:

Ocelot Facts: Find out cool things about ocelots and tell others. This helps more people learn about ocelots.

Heroes for Ocelots: Learn about people who work to save ocelots. Share their stories to show others how they can help, too.

Conclusion: Guardians of the Shadows — Ensuring a Future for the Ocelot

Ocelots, living quietly in the forests, face dangers. We have learned about their lives and how important it is to protect them.

A Shared Duty:

The ocelot's story tells us we all need to help keep them safe. We must work together to make sure they can live in the wild.

A Legacy of Care:

Like ocelot mothers teach their kittens, we should take care of the wild. If we help protect ocelots, we are helping our planet. Let us make sure these cats have a future, just like they help nature have a future.

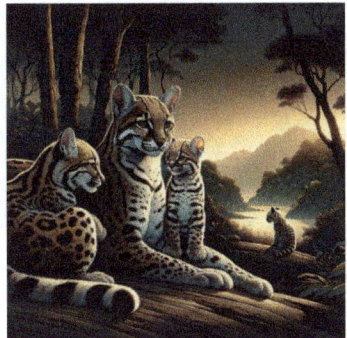

Glossary:

- The **Ocelot**, a beautiful wild cat with a patterned coat, inhabits the Americas.

- **Cubs** are baby ocelots that are taught and protected by their mothers.

- **Rainforest:** A dense, tropical forest where many ocelots live, full of diverse plants and animals.

- **Camouflage:** The ocelot's fur pattern helps it hide from predators and sneak up on prey.

- **Territory:** The specific area where an ocelot lives and hunts.

- **Conservation:** Actions to protect ocelots and their habitats from harm.

- **Solitary:** Ocelots mostly live alone, except when mothers are raising their cubs.

- **Nocturnal:** Ocelots are active at night, hunting and exploring.

- **Endangered:** Ocelots face threats that could make them disappear, like loss of habitat.

- **Habitat:** The natural home of an ocelot, which can be rainforests, grasslands, or marshes.

- **Stealth:** The careful, silent way ocelots move to catch prey or avoid danger.

CHAPTER 10:
SERVAL CHRONICLES:
MOTHERS OF THE
SAVANNAH

Introduction to the Serval

Graceful Grassland Dwellers:

Deep in Africa's wide grasslands, the serval moves with a beautiful and slender grace.

They wear a golden coat with dark spots and stripes and are known for their tall legs and lean bodies. Servals are a beautiful sight in the savannah, full of the wild's spirit.

Remarkable Ear Tufts and Hunting Prowess:

Servals have big, round ears with little black tufts on top. They can hear very well, which helps them find their food with great care. They can jump high to catch birds flying, showing off their quickness and agility. These features make them great hunters. They are also wonderful mothers who teach their little ones how to survive.

A Symbol of Adaptability:

Servals are good at living in many places. They range from dry savannas to marshy wetlands. They can handle many environments. This is important for keeping balance where they live. They are both hunters and hunted, and they help keep their home full of life and variety.

We are going to learn more about servals. They are skilled hunters and mothers in the African grasslands. We will see how being able to adapt and strong motherly love are both important in nature.

The Serval's Domain: Territory and Behavior

Territorial Mastery:

Servals have a powerful sense of their own space in the big grasslands. They mark their land with scents to show where their territory is. This helps them keep their hunting area safe, which is important for taking care of their young. They choose their territory carefully to make sure they have everything they need.

Adapting to the Clock:

Servals change their habits with the time of day. They blend in with the grass when the sun is up, and at night, their sharp senses help them hunt. They live two different ways, showing their cubs how to be smart and flexible in the savannah.

Mastery over Environment:

Servals teach their cubs how to be quiet and sneak around, so they learn to balance being seen and being hidden. These lessons are important for when the cubs grow up and live on their own in the big grasslands.

Birth and Early Life

Choosing the Den:

Serval mothers find secret places in
the grasslands to have their babies.
These safe dens protect the little ones
from danger when they are first born.

First Glimpse of Life:

Baby servals come into the world
blind and need their mom a lot. After a couple of weeks, they
start to see and explore near their den. Their mother watches
over them as they start their journey to becoming independent.

Growth and Exploration:

As time goes by, serval kittens play more, which helps them
learn how to hunt and stay safe. They follow their mom to learn
how to get around their grassland home.

Raising the Next Generation

Mastering the Hunt:

Serval moms are great teachers, showing their cubs how to hunt quietly. The cubs watch and learn how to move without making noise, getting ready for life in the wild.

From Play to Predation:

As they get bigger, the kittens' play turns into real hunting practice. They copy their mom and practice jumping and timing. This change is a big part of growing up for them, as they start to act like real hunters.

Independence on the Horizon:

With their mom watching, serval kittens become more independent. They start trying to hunt by themselves, using what their mom taught them. They get ready to go out and find their own place in the world.

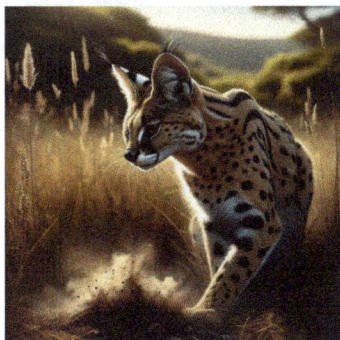

Lesser-Known Features and Behaviors

Communicating in the Grasslands:

Servals do not just hunt quietly; they also make different sounds to talk to each other. They purr softly to their family and can make loud calls across the grasslands. They also use scents to mark their territory. It is like drawing invisible lines to show where their land is.

Mastery of Marking:

Marking their territory is important for servals. They use scents to let other servals know where they live. This helps them avoid fights and keep things peaceful in the savannah.

Leaps and Bounds:

Servals can leap high to catch birds in the air. This shows how well they can move and hunt. They have strong legs and muscles, which makes them unique hunters.

These lesser-known parts of a serval's life show how interesting it is. They also show how adaptable they are. Their way of talking, marking their land, and hunting skills make them important. They are key for life in the African grasslands.

The Path to Adulthood

Early Independence:

As serval kittens get older, they start learning to live by themselves on the African plains. They practice being sneaky and getting to know their home, which is all part of becoming an adult.

Lessons in the Savannah:

Young servals get better at hunting with their mom's help. When they can hunt on their own, it is a sign that they are ready for life by themselves.

Solitary Journeys:

Eventually, servals leave their family to live alone. They find their own territory and start their own life. This is a big step for them and shows how strong and able to change they are.

Servals' journey to adulthood is a mix of what they are born knowing and what they learn from their mom. When they become adults, they are ready to help keep the grasslands balanced and full of life.

Conservation Efforts and Impact

Challenges to Survival:

Servals are beautiful and graceful. But, they face big problems. They lose their homes to farms or are hunted. These threats can upset the balance of their grassland homes and make it hard for them to survive.

Conservation Initiatives:

People are working to help servals. They keep their homes safe. They stop illegal hunting and study their needs. Protecting wildlife and the laws that keep them safe are important. They keep servals and their environment secure.

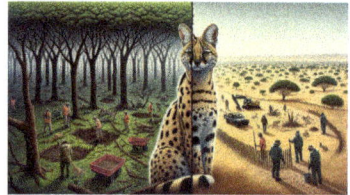

Ecological Balance:

Servals are important in nature. They help control the number of other animals and keep their homes healthy. Protecting them is key for the grasslands to stay balanced and full of diverse kinds of life.

Saving servals is not just about protecting one species. It is also about caring for the whole ecosystem. By supporting these efforts, we can ensure servals keep living in their natural homes. This will keep the grasslands of Africa healthy and diverse.

The Legacy of Serval Mothers

Maternal Mastery:

Serval moms are good at taking care of their babies. They teach them what they need to know to make it in the wild. Their hard work makes sure the next generation can live well in the African plains.

Symbols of Adaptability:

These moms show us how to manage life's challenges with grace. Their story is about the strength of nature and the power of motherly love in the wild.

Guardians of the Grasslands:

By teaching and protecting their little ones, serval moms help keep the balance in nature. Their legacy is seen in how well their babies do. They keep servals as a part of Africa's landscapes.

The story of serval moms is about more than just staying alive. It shows how caring for each other is key to the health and future of all creatures. Their ability to change, be strong, and care for their little ones is a lesson in the wonder and design of nature.

Engaging with Serval Serenades

Creative Discovery:

Make a Model of a Serval Home: Using things you can recycle, build a model of where servals live. Add things like tall grass, water, and a hidden spot for sleeping to show the serval's perfect home.

Pretend You're a Serval: Think up a story about a day in the life of a serval. Act out hunting in the grasslands. Stay safe from danger and look after babies. Do this to show what life is like for servals.

Championing Conservation:

Create a Club for Wildlife. Get together with friends to learn about servals and other animals near you. Share what you learn and think of ways to help save local wildlife.

Send letters to groups that save wildlife. In the letters, show your support for saving servals. Tell others about what you learn by posting online or talking at school.

Discovery and Sharing:

Fun Facts Game: Look up interesting things about servals. Share them in a fun way, like a quiz or a poster, to teach and excite others.

Art for Animals: Use your creativity to show why it is important to save servals. Share your art online or at events to help others understand and care about saving their homes.

By doing these fun activities, kids and grown-ups can learn more about servals. They can also take part in saving them. Getting to know these mysterious cats teaches us. It also connects us to the natural world. This helps us become champions for conservation.

Preserving the Serval Legacy

Graceful Guardians of the Grasslands:

Think about how serval moms are so important in the African grasslands. They teach their babies how to live and make sure their kind keeps going. Their smooth way of handling life shows us the careful balance in the savannah.

A Call to Action:

Show how everyone can help keep these amazing animals and their homes safe. Encourage people to do things. They should support groups that protect wildlife. They should also back groups that fight for the safety of grassland homes.

Inspiring Future Guardians:

Motivate readers to become protectors of animals, showing that every little bit helps. We can learn about and respect serval moms and their world. This can lead to better ways for all creatures to live together.

We dive into the story of serval moms and their cubs. It invites us to love and understand nature. We feel a duty to save it and promise to protect our shared world forever.

Glossary:

- **Serval:** A medium-sized African cat known for its long legs and large ears.

- **Kittens:** Young servals learning to hunt and survive in the wild.

- **Grassland:** Open, grassy areas where servals live and hunt.

- **Ears:** Servals have large ears to hear small prey moving in the grass.

- **Leap:** Servals can jump high into the air to catch birds.

- **Camouflage:** Their spotted coat helps servals hide from both prey and predators.

- **Solitary:** Servals live and hunt alone, marking their

territory with scent.

- **Conservation:** Protecting servals and their habitats to ensure their survival.

- **Predator:** Servals hunt smaller animals for food, using their speed and agility.

- **Nocturnal:** Servals are most active at night when hunting.

- **Territory:** The area a serval defends and considers its own for hunting.

- **Adaptation:** Servals have adapted to their environment with long legs for jumping and large ears for hearing.

CHAPTER 11: WHISPERS OF THE FOREST: THE AFRICAN GOLDEN CAT

Introduction to the African Golden Cat

Elusive Shadows: The African Golden Cat Unveiled

It lives in Africa's thick rainforests. The cat is hidden there. It is called the African Golden Cat (Profelis aurata).

Its fur can be golden, reddish-brown, or gray, and it is one of Africa's most mysterious wild cats. These cats are truly wild, but we do not

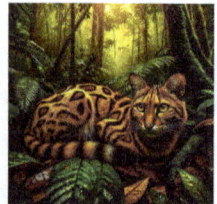

know much about them because they are so
hard to find.

Realm of the Rainforest: A Habitat Defined

The African Golden Cat calls the complicated world of the rainforest its home. Here, in Central and West Africa's jungles, the
cat has learned to find its way and thrive. The forest protects it
and gives it a place to hunt. It shows its great climbing skills
and love for thick plants. This shows how well it fits into its
home, living with the rainforest.

Master of Adaptation: Survival in the Green

The African Golden Cat is amazing at
living in the rainforest. Its fur helps it
hide in the patches of light and shadow, and being alone means less fighting for food. This cat's life shows us
how a predator and its home must
stay in balance. It also shows how vital the African Golden Cat is to the life
of the tropical forest.

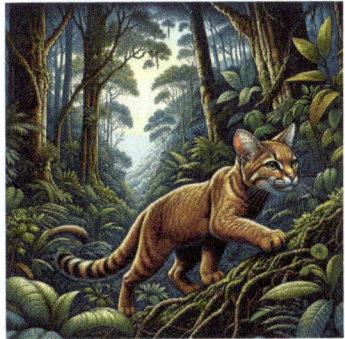

Birth and Early Days

Secluded Beginnings: The First Steps of Life

In the quiet parts of Africa's rainforests, African Golden Cat cubs
start their lives. They are born hidden away, in thick plants or old
logs. Their mother looks after them
carefully. The first few weeks are all
about staying safe and growing, far
from any dangers.

Awakening to the Wild: Early Lessons Amongst the Green

As the cubs get bigger, they start to see more of the world
with their mother's help. They take small steps into their
green home, getting to know the place where they will hunt
one day. This is not just about walking around; it is the start
of learning how to live in the wild. They learn about finding
shelter and listening to the sounds of the forest.

Raising the Next Generation

Mastering the Shadows: The Art of Stealth and Survival

In the heart of the rainforest, the
mother cat is teaching her cubs how
to live. She shows them how to move
without being seen, listen to the quiet sounds, and understand their prey.

These lessons are about more than hunting; they are about becoming a part of the forest itself.

From Dependence to Mastery: The Journey Toward Independence

The cubs learn more every day as they get ready to live on their own. They practice hunting and learn to find their way through the forest. Big moments, like their first catch, show they are growing up. The mother cat watches and helps them become clever hunters who can take care of themselves.

This time of growing up is careful and full of the mother's wisdom. She knows when to lead and when to let her cubs learn on their own. Her teaching makes sure the cubs can manage the rainforest when they are ready to go out alone. They grow up with the skills to survive and keep their kind going in the whispers of the forest.

Family Bonds and Social Dynamics

Nurturing Bonds: The Maternal Connection

The bond between the African Golden Cat mother and her cubs is deep and caring. It is all about keeping the little ones safe and healthy. The mother is there for them from the moment they are born until they are ready to be on their own. This bond changes as the cubs grow, but the love and lessons they get will always be a part of them.

Path to Independence: Embracing Solitude

Growing up means the cubs start to wander further away and learn how to be alone. The mother cat changes from caring for them up close to watching from afar. Her cubs practice living on their own, learning from their successes and mistakes. This change from being young and needing help to being an adult and living alone is important. It makes sure each cat can find and keep its own place in the big rainforest.

The African Golden Cat shows us how important it is to balance being together and having space to grow. This balance lets the cats live well and keep having new generations. Each new cat learns from its family. It does so until it is ready to live in the quiet forest and keep the family traditions alive.

Lesser-Known Features and Behaviors

Masters of Camouflage

The African Golden Cat is a wizard of disguise in the thick forests of Central and West Africa. It has a coat of colors that look like the forest floor. This makes it invisible to both its prey and bigger animals that might hunt it. This camouflage is a key part of how it survives, not just for hunting.

Whispers of the Wild: Communication in Silence

Even though they are hard to find, African Golden Cats have their own ways of making sounds to talk to each other. They can growl deeply, hiss softly, or even meow gently. The noises create a secret language. It lets them share feelings, plans, and info. This way of talking is important for mothers and cubs to stay in touch in the thick forest. These sounds, often too quiet for us to hear, are a big part of their hidden social life in the rainforest.

It is good at hiding and has a unique way of talking. This lets the African Golden Cat live fully in the rainforest. These secret parts of its life show an animal perfectly suited to its home. It is full of the wonder and wildness of the African rainforest.

Conservation Efforts and Impact

A Rainforest at Risk

The future of the African Golden Cat is uncertain. Its rainforest home is being cut down, broken up, and hunted in ways that are not sustainable. These problems are shrinking the forest and harming the web of life that the cat depends on. People who want to save these cats work hard. They are working to protect the rainforests of Central and West Africa. They are making sure hunting is done right. They are protecting certain areas. They are also promoting ways to use the land without harming it.

Pioneering Protection Through Research

Learning about the African Golden Cat is hard because it hides so well. So, research is important for saving it. Scientists and animal protectors are using camera traps. They are studying animals in the wild. They are also getting local people involved. They want to learn how many animals there are, how they behave, and where they live. This information is needed to produce good plans to save them. Protecting their rainforest home is more important than ever. Research and protection must work together to keep the African Golden Cat living free in the wild.

They are trying to keep the African Golden Cat safe. They want to save the environment. They also aim to protect the many forms of life in its rainforest home. These efforts show how important it is for all to unite. They must unite against environmental threats. They show the key role of research, protection, and getting everyone involved. Their goal is to keep one of Africa's most secret wild cats living in the wild.

The Legacy of the African Golden Cat

Forest Sentinels

The African Golden Cat is a silent guardian in the rich rainforests of Central and West Africa. It plays a big part in keeping the forest balanced. As a hunter, it helps control the number of other animals. This keeps the forest healthy and full of various kinds of life. When you see this cat, it means the forest is doing well. It is a key part of the rainforest world. Its secret life and perfect fit in the dense forest show us the mystery and beauty of these green places. They remind us how everything in nature is connected.

A Rallying Cry for Conservation

The story of the African Golden Cat is a strong call to save the African rainforests. It asks us to see how everything in life is linked. We must protect these places from being cut, broken, and other dangers. Saving the rainforest keeps a home for the African Golden Cat. It also helps many other species and the vital things these forests do for us. Let the quiet sound of the African Golden Cat in the trees inspire us. It should inspire us to promise to save these vital places for the future.

In thinking about the African Golden Cat's legacy, we are asked to love and care for the rich life there. By supporting efforts to save these places, we can keep the secret sound of the African Golden Cat in the forest. This shows how much we care about keeping our natural world safe.

Challenges and Adaptations

Navigating the Rainforest

Life in the rainforest is not easy for the African Golden Cat. They must compete with other animals for food. They must also stay away from bigger predators, like leopards. The seasons change, and so does the food they can find, so they must be smart about how they hunt all year round.

Mastering Adaptations

The African Golden Cat has become good at living in the rainforest. It's great at climbing and moving in trees. Being active at night helps it hunt without running into other predators or having to share its food.

The Art of Stealth

Being sneaky is the most important way the African Golden Cat stays safe and finds food. Its fur blends in with the ground, and it moves so quietly that it is almost invisible. It waits patiently and then pounces on its food with perfect timing.

The challenges and the cat's ways to overcome them show how tough and clever the African Golden Cat is. It can stay hidden, move gracefully, and blend with its environment. This makes it important in the rainforest life of Central and West Africa.

Conclusion—A Tribute to the African Golden Cat Mother

Guardians of the Green

The mother African Golden Cat lives deep in Africa's rainforests. She is a symbol of the strength and wisdom of the wild. She is very dedicated to her cubs. She chooses the safest places for them to live and teaches them all they need to know to survive. These mothers are the true champions of the rainforest. They show the toughness and adaptability that define the African Golden Cat.

Legacy of the Forest

The work of the African Golden Cat mother does more than keep her cubs alive. It helps keep the whole rainforest alive and well. She is not just preparing her cubs for life. She is also making sure that the cats that come after them can live in the ecosystem. This keeps things balanced.

A Call to Action

Honoring the African Golden Cat mother also means we need to act. It reminds us how important it is to protect the rainforest and all the living things there. We help the African Golden Cat by protecting its habitat. This helps it and many other creatures live there. Let us let the challenging work of these cat moms inspire us. It should inspire us to protect their home. We must keep the secrets of the forest safe for many years to come.

Glossary:

- **African Golden Cat:** A rare wild cat that lives in the rainforests of Central and West Africa, known for its beautiful golden or reddish-brown fur.

- **Rainforest:** A dense, wet forest found near the equator, home to many plants and animals, including the African Golden Cat.

- **Camouflage:** The way animals blend into their surroundings to hide from predators or sneak up on prey; the African Golden Cat's fur helps it hide in the forest.

- **Cubs:** Baby African Golden Cats that learn to survive in the forest with their mother's help.

- **Stealth:** Moving quietly and carefully to avoid being seen or heard; an important skill for hunting or staying hidden.

- **Conservation:** Efforts to protect and preserve wild animals and their natural habitats from harm.

- **Ecosystem:** A community of living things, including plants and animals, which interact with each other and their environment.

- **Predator:** An animal that hunts and eats other animals for food. The African Golden Cat is a predator in the rainforest.

- **Solitude:** The state of being alone or isolated; African Golden Cats often live and hunt alone, except for mothers with cubs.

- **Territory:** An area that an animal, like the African Golden Cat, claims as its own and defends against others of its kind.

CHAPTER 12: SHADOWS OF THE EAST: THE ASIAN GOLDEN CAT

Introduction to the Asian Golden Cat

A Mysterious Feline of Asia

The Asian Golden Cat lives deep in the forests and rugged mountains of Southeast and East Asia. Its life is hidden from view.

This medium-sized wild cat, with fur that can be golden, brown, or gray, is an expert in hiding. It is not as well-known as the bigger wild cats, but it is just as fascinating.

Master of Adaptation

The Asian Golden Cat can live in many different places, from hot, wet rainforests to cold, high forests. In every place, it fits in perfectly with the world around it, showing how tough and flexible it is.

A Creature of Beauty and Mystery

The life of the Asian Golden Cat is a reminder of how amazing and hidden nature can be. As we learn more about this cat, we see how well it fits into Asia's many ecosystems. We also understand more about the secrets and depth of the natural world.

First Steps in the Wild: The Asian Golden Cat's Early Journey

Hidden Beginnings

Asian Golden Cats start their lives hidden away in the wild, in thick plants or under rocks. Here, the mother cat gives birth. She cares for her cubs, protecting them from danger and giving them a safe start in life.

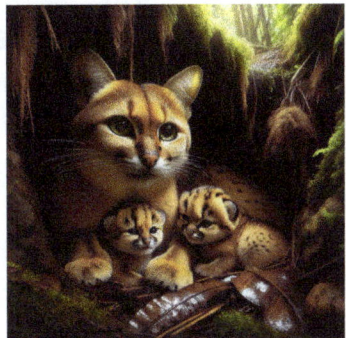

First Steps into a Larger World

The cubs soon start to explore, guided by their mother. They play and learn about the world, getting ready for the day they will master their wild home. Their mother's teachings help them not just to survive but to really thrive in Asia's wild places.

Raising the Next Generation: The Asian Golden Cat's Path to Independence

Mastering Survival Skills

In the lush forests of Southeast Asia, mother Asian Golden Cats teach their cubs all they need to know. They teach them all they need to know to survive. They show them how to hide, move without being seen, and hunt for food.

The Journey to Independence

The cubs grow up, getting braver and more skilled. They start to hunt on their own, getting ready to find their own place in the forest. Their mother watches, ready to help but knowing they need to learn to live on their own.

The lessons these cubs learn are the keys to their future. They learn to live and do well in their home, getting ready to keep their species going in the Asian wilderness.

Family Bonds and Social Dynamics

Maternal Bonds: Nurturing the Future

The bond between an Asian Golden Cat mother and her cubs is strong and full of care. She teaches, protects, and gets them ready for the day they will live on their own.

Solitary Nature: A Life Apart

Asian Golden Cats usually live alone. They find their own territories and keep them safe. They only come together with other cats to mate, then go back to living alone. Growing up means learning to take care of themselves and live independently.

Feline Mysteries Unraveled: The Asian Golden Cat's Hidden Traits

Nature's Palette: Coat Variations

The Asian Golden Cat's fur can be many colors, which helps it survive and talk to other cats. The fur colors help it hide or show other cats that it is time to mate or to stay away.

Silent Communications: Marking and Vocalizing

These cats use smells to mark their territory and sometimes make quiet sounds to talk to each other. They mostly live alone. But, they have ways to tell other cats about important things. These things include mating or territory.

The Language of Camouflage

The cat's fur helps it stay hidden. This is key for catching food and staying safe from other animals.

Territories and Whispers

Asian Golden Cats are like quiet guardians of their land. They use smells and sounds to make their home and talk to other cats. This shows how deeply they are connected to their territory.

Guardianship in Peril: Protecting the Asian Golden Cat

A Precarious Existence

The Asian Golden Cat's journey to survive is fraught with danger. Humans are moving deeper into the cats' territories. They are destroying habitats and poaching. This pushes the cats closer to the edge of extinction. Once, they roamed freely in large forests. Now, they find their homes shrinking and split.

Conservation's Frontline

They joined forces to fend off extinction. The group includes conservationists, researchers, and lawmakers. Their mission is to create safe havens for the Asian Golden Cat. They will also enforce laws against poaching. They will also help people and wildlife live together peacefully. International treaties like CITES defend against the illegal wildlife trade. They are a beacon of hope for the cat's future.

The Catalyst of Research

Research is the backbone of conservation. It gives us the knowledge we need to protect the Asian Golden Cat well. Understanding these cats' behaviors, social structures, and interactions with the environment is key. It will help us create conservation strategies. These strategies will protect the cats and the ecosystems they are part of.

Every bit of progress is a victory. Every protected area and changed heart for conservation is too. They are victories in the battle to save the Asian Golden Cat. We join for conservation. We are inspired by the recognition that we are preserving nature itself. We see the true power of working together.

The Legacy of the Asian Golden Cat

Protectors of Diversity: Guardians of the Forest

The Asian Golden Cat is a shadowy figure in the forests of the East. It is key to keeping the balance of its ecosystem. It is a top predator. It keeps the number of smaller creatures in check. This is crucial for a healthy and diverse forest.

A Call to Preserve: Safeguarding Their Future

The fate of the Asian Golden Cat is tied to the fate of its forest home. These cats are more than forest residents—they are a symbol of wildness and complexity. Their presence is a sign of a healthy ecosystem, which is essential for the health of our planet. As we witness their homes and numbers dwindle, the call to protect them becomes more urgent.

Conserving the Asian Golden Cat means protecting an entire world of life. Conservation efforts must focus on three things. They are keeping habitats intact. They stop poaching and help humans and wildlife live in peace.

As we think about the legacy of the Asian Golden Cat, let us commit to conservation. Let us make sure future generations can marvel at these cats' grace and mystery. Together, we can make sure they keep wandering free, a symbol of the wild's enduring spirit.

The Asian Golden Cat's Trail: Activities for Young Explorers

Interactive Exploration and Creative Engagement

Explore the world of the Asian Golden Cat. Do activities that spark curiosity and promote conservation. They range from art projects to research. These activities connect you to the life of one of Asia's most elusive wild cats.

Creative Activities

Jungle Canvas: Paint or draw the Asian Golden Cat's homes. Capture the beauty of the forests where they live.

Day in the Life Diary: Write about a day as an Asian Golden Cat. Describe the challenges and beauty they experience every day.

Golden Cat Masks: Create a mask showing the cat's unique fur patterns. Use different materials to mimic their colorful coats.

Conservation in Action

Guardians of the Forest: Learn about the Asian Golden Cat's conservation status. Share what you find to raise awareness about their situation.

Write to organizations or governments, which support the Asian Golden Cat. Explain why it is important to protect these cats.

Eco-Art Exhibition: Host an art show about the Asian Golden Cat and its home. Teach others about the importance of saving these cats.

Discover and Share

A unique section will provide resources to learn more about the Asian Golden Cat. Check out websites, documentaries, and conservation programs dedicated to keeping Asia's wildlife safe.

By engaging in these activities, you help protect the Asian Golden Cat and its home. Let your creativity and passion guide you to a brighter future for these beautiful cats.

Cultural Echoes: The Asian Golden Cat

Mythical Guardian

In Southeast and East Asian folklore, the Asian Golden Cat is a figure of wonder. Seen as a guardian of forests and a sign of good luck, it shows how meaningful it is to these cultures.

Coexistence Through Time

Humans and the Asian Golden Cat have a long history. They are part of the spirit and nature in many stories. This reminds us to respect these old ties in our conservation efforts.

Artistic Inspirations

The mystery of the Asian Golden Cat inspires many stories and art. Its image in culture is a reminder of its heritage. It shows the importance of protecting this living symbol of wild beauty.

By mixing tradition with conservation, we learn to value our natural heritage. We work for a future where people and the environment cooperate.

Conclusion: Guardians of the Shadows—Ensuring a Future for the Asian Golden Cat

The Asian Golden Cat is a hidden symbol of the biodiversity of Southeast and East Asia. It needs our protection. As threats to its survival grow, we must step up as guardians of the natural world. Saving the forests and wilderness areas saves the Asian Golden Cat. It saves all the life connected to it. Let this be our call to action—a reminder that the fate of these secretive creatures is in our hands. We can work together. We can make sure the Asian Golden Cat stays roaming free. It is a beacon of the wild's lasting spirit.

Glossary:

Asian Golden Cat: A medium-sized wild cat with fur that can be golden, brown, or gray, found in Southeast and East Asia's forests and mountains.

Adaptation: The process by which animals change over time to better survive in their environments; the Asian Golden Cat is adapted to live in various habitats.

Coexistence: Living together in the same area without causing harm to each other; efforts to promote coexistence between Asian Golden Cats and humans are important for conservation.

Habitat: The natural environment where an animal lives; Asian Golden Cats can live in rainforests, grasslands, and mountains.

Camouflage: The Asian Golden Cat's fur helps it blend into its surroundings, making it an effective hunter.

Conservation: Protecting and preserving natural resources and the environment; conservation efforts are crucial for the Asian Golden Cat's survival.

Ecosystem: The Asian Golden Cat plays a role in its ecosystem by helping control the population of its prey.

Independence: Asian Golden Cat cubs learn to live independently from their mother as they grow older.

Poaching: Illegal hunting, which is a threat to the Asian Golden Cat; conservation efforts aim to combat poaching.

Territorial: Describes how Asian Golden Cats claim and defend a specific area as their own.

CHAPTER 13: THE ENIGMATIC PALLAS'S CAT: A PORTRAIT OF MOTHERHOOD IN THE

Welcome to the World of the Pallas's Cat

The Secret Mountain Cat

Deep in the wild lands of Central Asia, there is a unique cat with a lot of fluff called the Pallas's Cat.

This cat looks like it is always frowning and lives where it is very cold and high up in the mountains. It has thick fur to keep warm and a body that is right for living in such a place. A smart man named Peter Simon Pallas discov-

ered this cat. Few people know much about it. This is because it likes to hide and be alone.

The Land of Grass and Hills

The Pallas's Cat makes its home in the big grassy areas and hills of Central Asia. The land is tough to live in with cold mountains and windy flat lands. But this cat knows how to manage it all by itself. It finds food and travels around its home, which is a big part of nature in this part of the world.

Choosing a Home for Little Cats

The Mother Cat's Perfect Choice

Mother Pallas's Cats pick the best spots for their babies to be born. They like to use rocky holes or places dug by other animals. They use them to keep their kittens safe from the cold and other danger-ous animals. The first part of the kittens' lives is spent in these cozy hidden spots, with their mother taking care of them.

Cozy Beginnings for the Kittens

The kittens stay in their warm den for the first few weeks. They cannot see and need their mother a lot. This time is important for eating and growing strong. They stay safe in their den until they are ready to see the world outside.

Stepping into the Big World

Soon, the kittens follow their mother out of the den to see the big grassy lands that will be their home. They are careful but curious, learning about all the new things they see, hear, and smell. Playing and learning at the same time is important for them to know how to live in their new home.

Teaching How to Be a Wild Cat

Learning to Stay Safe and Find Food

The mother cat has a big job teaching her kittens how to find food and stay safe in the open land. She shows them how to sneak up on what they want to catch and wait for the right time to jump. Learning to hide and hunt is important for them.

Growing Up and Getting Ready

The kittens get better at hunting and start to feel sure of themselves. They watch their mother and try to do what she does. They learn to understand the land and start to be more independent. This is how they get ready to live on their own one day.

Becoming Their Own Boss

When the kittens are ready, they start to live by themselves, which is what Pallas's Cats do. They use what their mother taught them to take care of themselves. Now they are grown up and can look after their own piece of the big, wild land.

Family Time and How Cats Grow Up

Caring for the Future: A Mother's Love

In the wild lands of Central Asia, the love between a mother Pallas's cat and her babies is important. The mom works hard to keep her little ones safe and teach them how to live in the tough world outside. She picks the best hiding spots for them to live in and shows them what they need to know to grow up strong. This time with their mom helps the kittens learn to be brave and ready for their own adventures.

Learning to Be Alone: Getting Ready for Grown-Up Life

Even though grown-up Pallas's cats like to be alone, they start their lives close to their family. Playing and spending time with brothers, sisters, and their mom teaches them how to get along. It teaches them to share and be by themselves. As they get bigger, they start to do more things on their own. This change happens slowly and naturally. They have been taught well and are ready to live alone. It shows that the mom did a fantastic job in raising her kittens.

The Circle of Life Keeps Going

When the young Pallas's cats start their own lives, the story of life in their home goes on. They use what their mom taught them to manage the challenges they face. Later, they will find mates and have kittens. They will make sure there are more Pallas's cats in the future. The strong bond between the mom and her kittens is clear as each new group of cats continues the family story.

Hiding in Plain Sight: How Cats Stay Safe

Being Sneaky to Survive

Pallas's cats are good at hiding because they look like the land around them. Their fur matches the colors and shapes of where they live, so it is hard for other animals to see them. They move carefully and quietly so they will not be noticed. This skill is impor-

tant because it helps them stay safe and find food without being seen.

Talking Without Being Seen

Even though they usually like to be alone, Pallas's cats have unique ways of making sounds to talk to each other. They make quiet noises to talk to their babies or louder sounds if they meet other adult cats. These sounds help the mom and kittens stay together and understand each other. During the time when they are looking for a partner, these sounds help them find each other. All these different noises are an important part of how Pallas's cats live and have babies.

Working Together to Keep Cats Safe

The Challenge of Staying Safe

The beautiful Pallas's cats have problems. People and other dangers are changing their homes. Their land is getting broken up by too many animals eating the grass or people digging for things in the ground. Some people also catch cats for their fur or to use in medicine. But animal lovers are trying to help. They are making safe places for the cats. They are also making rules against catching them. And they are learning more to help protect them.

Everyone Helping Out

People from all over the world are working together to help save Pallas's cats. They are counting how many cats there are. They are fixing up their homes. They are also helping people learn why it is important to keep cats safe. By working together, people hope to save the cats. They also want to save the place where the cats live. They want to do this so that the cats can stay around for a long time.

The Mom Cat's Important Job

The Keeper of the Grasslands

Mother Pallas's cat has a big job in the wide grassy lands of Central Asia. She takes diligent care of her kittens and teaches them everything they need to know. Her hard work is a sign of how tough and smart these cats are. The mom cat is like a hero of the wild places where they live, making sure her kittens can keep the family going.

Helping to Save the Land

The story of the mom cat and her kittens is more than about them. The big open land they live on is important for lots of plants and animals, not just cats. Keeping this place safe means we must work hard. We must stop it from being ruined and people from catching cats. We must also help with changes in the weather. Let us all help take care of the animals and their homes so that they can stay wonderful and wild.

Fun Ways to Learn about Pallas's Cats

Make a Mini Home

This activity is to build a small model of where Pallas's cats live. Use things like grass, small stones, and cloth to look like the land. Add a tiny cat figure to finish your project. This helps you see where these cats live and why we need to protect them.

Speak Up for the Cats

Activity: Help Pallas's cats by telling other people about their needs and how we can keep them safe. You can do a project at school or tell your friends and family how to help save the cats and their grassy homes. Your work can make a real difference.

Learn and Share Facts

Task: Find out cool things about Pallas's cats. Learn how they handle the cold, catch their food, and live where they do. Make a poster or a computer slideshow to show your class, friends, or family. Sharing this info helps more people care. It is about these unique cats and their homes.The Pallas's Cat in Stories and Traditions

The Magical Cat of the Mountains

In the wild mountains of Central Asia, there is a fluffy cat called the Pallas's Cat, or Manul. It is a unique cat that people have told stories about for many years. The stories say the Pallas's Cat is like a magical animal. It has learned to live alone and manage harsh weather. The tales of Pallas's Cat are full of wonder. They make people think of a cat that is part of the earth but also has something unique. We cannot quite understand it.

Why Stories Matter for Keeping Cats Safe

The Pallas's Cat is important in the stories and traditions of the people who live where the cat does. It is like a symbol of the wild and free spirit of the mountains and grasslands. Using these stories can help people want to keep Pallas's Cat safe. We can connect with people through their own cat stories. Then, everyone can work together to protect the cat and its home.

Cats in Art

Artists have always liked to make pictures and stories about the Pallas's Cat. It looks different from other cats, and people are curious about it. They make art, write stories, and even make movies about this cat. When people make these, they help others learn about the Pallas's Cat. They also learn why it is important to keep it safe.

Keeping Stories Alive

Telling stories about the Pallas's Cat is an effective way to help keep it safe. When we share the old legends and tales about the cat, we keep the history and traditions alive. At the same time, we show why the Pallas's Cat is important to the land and all the living things there. This can make people care more about the land and the animals and want to take care of them.

A Tribute to the Mother Cat

The mother Pallas's Cat in the big, quiet grasslands is a sign of strength, mystery, and the free spirit of nature. Her life shows how hard and beautiful it can be to live in a tough place. She works hard to take care of her babies and teach them how to live on their own. Her story is part of the land itself, and she helps keep the future safe.

Remembering the Mother Cat and Her Home

Thinking about the mother Pallas's Cat can inspire us to take care
of the place where she lives. As we
admire how strong these mother
cats are, we should also remember that we need to protect their
home. This matters not just for the
cats. It also keeps the stories and
traditions. They have honored these mysterious animals for so
long.

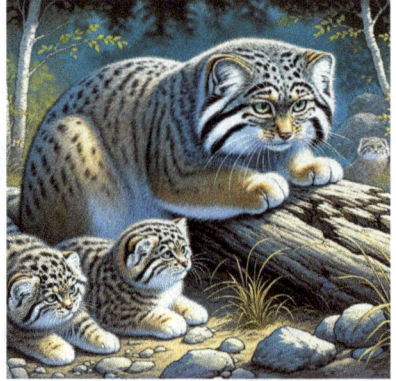

Mother Pallas's Cat's story, passed down through time, reminds us to help keep the cats safe. We look after the grasslands. We speak up for Pallas's Cat. This shows respect for a
creature that has amazed people for years. Let us promise to
keep the wonder and strength of the Pallas's Cat alive. This
way, their soft sounds can still be heard in the grasslands' wind.
We will honor the wild spirit in all of us.

Glossary:

- **Pallas's Cat:** A small, fluffy wild cat found in the grasslands and mountainous regions of Central Asia, known
  for its distinctive facial expression.

- **Grasslands:** Large open areas of land covered with
  grass, where Pallas's Cat often lives and hunts.

- **Mountainous Regions:** Areas with high mountains,

which are part of the Pallas's Cat's natural habitat.

- **Thick Fur:** The Pallas's Cat has thick fur that helps protect it from cold temperatures in its high-altitude home.

- **Solitary:** Pallas's Cats are mostly solitary, meaning they prefer to live and hunt alone.

- **Cubs:** Young Pallas's Cats that are raised by their mother in a den before learning to navigate their environment.

- **Stealth and Survival:** Pallas's Cats are masters of stealth, using their skills to hunt prey and avoid predators.

- **Conservation Status:** The level of threat to a species; Pallas's Cats are considered near threatened, meaning they could become endangered without conservation efforts.

- **Ecosystem Role:** Pallas's Cats play a crucial role in their ecosystem by controlling the populations of certain prey species.

- **Adaptations:** Physical or behavioral changes that allow an animal to survive in its environment; Pallas's Cats have several adaptations for cold climates and solitary living.

CHAPTER 14: WATERSIDE WHISKERS: THE FISHING CAT'S TALE

Welcome to the World of the Fishing Cat

The Cat Who Loves to Swim

Imagine a cat who lives in the wet and wild places of South and Southeast Asia.

This is the Fishing Cat, and it has a strong body and unique feet that help it swim very well. It can catch fish easily, and its fur keeps it warm and dry as it moves through the water. This cat is amazing at living in the water.

The Home of the Fishing Cat

Fishing Cats live where there is a lot of water. This includes forests with many trees near water, grassy areas with tall reeds, and swamps. These places are important for the Fishing Cat because it needs them to find food and live well. The cat helps keep everything in balance by eating fish and other small creatures in the water. Protecting these wet places is important for the Fishing Cat. It is also important for all the other animals and plants that live there.

First Steps and Swims

A Safe Place for Little Fishers

A mother Fishing Cat finds the perfect spot for her babies near the water. It is hidden and safe, so the baby cats can be cozy and protected. The mom takes great care of them there. Being near the water is important. It helps the baby cats start to learn about their life in and around the water.

Learning to Love the Water

When Fishing Cat kittens start to explore, their mom shows them how to swim. The first swims are crucial. They help the kittens get ready for their life in the wetlands. They practice swimming and catching things in the water, and their mom is always there to help them learn.

Growing Up to Catch Fish

Learning to Hunt

The mother Fishing Cat teaches her kittens how to find food in the water. They watch her and try to do the same thing. She shows them how to watch the water and catch fish at just the right time. The kittens have fun and learn a lot while they practice these skills.

Becoming Big Cats

As the kittens grow up, they get better at swimming and hunting. They start to do more on their own, and their mom watches to make sure they are ready to live by themselves. When they are big enough, they will go off to live their own lives, just like their mom taught them.

The Unique Bond with Mom

A Mother's Hard Work

The Fishing Cat mom works hard to take care of her kittens. She keeps them safe and teaches them everything they need to know about living in the wetlands. This care helps the kittens grow up to be strong and able to take care of themselves.

Becoming Independent

Even though they spend a lot of time with their mom as kittens, Fishing Cat kittens will one day live alone. The mom helps them get ready for this by slowly teaching them to be more independent. They learn how to take care of themselves, and soon they are ready to start their own adventures.

The Secret Life of the Fishing Cat

Nighttime Hunters

When the sun goes down, the Fishing Cat becomes a silent hunter in the dark. It uses the night to sneak up on fish and other animals in the water. The Fishing Cat's senses are very sharp, and it can notice even the smallest splash. Hunting at night helps the Fishing Cat catch food when other animals are not around.

Talking Softly in the Wild

Fishing Cats have their own quiet way of talking to each other. They do this between mothers and kittens. They use soft sounds that are hard for people to hear to stay in touch while hiding in the grass or reeds. This quiet talking helps them learn to hunt and stay safe together.

Keeping Wetlands Safe

Wetlands in Danger

The places where Fishing Cats live are being hurt. They are being changed by things like buildings, farming, and dirty water. Wetlands are important because they are full of life and help clean the water. If we lose these places, it is bad for the Fishing Cats and all the other animals and plants that need them to live.

Working Together for the Water

Many people all over the world are trying to save the wetlands where Fishing Cats live. They make safe places for the cats, take care of the land and water, and teach people how to help. When these places get better, it gives us hope that we can save the wetlands and the Fishing Cats.

A Guardian of the Marshes

The Fishing Cat is like a protector of the wetlands. It shows us that these places are healthy and full of life. When we help the Fishing Cat, we also help the whole wetland and every-thing that lives there.

A Call to Help the Wetlands

The story of the Fishing Cat tells us how important it is to take care of wetlands all over the world. We all need to work together to keep these places safe for the Fishing Cat and all the other living things. When we save the wetlands, we keep the story of the Fishing Cat alive for the future.

Fun Activities to Learn About Fishing Cats

Make a Wetland World

Activity: Create a small wetland in a box with dirt, rocks, plants, and water. Put in some toy Fishing Cats and other animals that live there. This helps us see where Fishing Cats live and why we should take care of wetlands.

Help Clean the Wetlands

Activity: Help clean up wetlands near you or start your own clean-up day. This helps the Fishing Cat's home and teaches people about how important wetlands are.

Study Wetland Animals

Activity: Find out about animals that live in wetlands, like the Fishing Cat. Show what you learn in a fun way, like a poster or a school project, to tell others about these animals.

Tell Others About Wetlands

Activity: Make posters or online posts about Fishing Cats. Show the problems their homes face. Share them to let others know how they can help save wetlands.

Write About Wetlands

Activity: Keep a journal or blog about the wetlands you see or learn about. Write about the animals, why these places matter, and what we can do to protect them.

Support Groups That Help Wetlands

Activity: Learn about groups that work to save wetlands and Fishing Cats. Find out how you can help them by giving support, telling others, or helping.

By doing these activities, kids and adults can enter the world of the Fishing Cat. They can also explore the wetlands where the cats live. These projects and actions help us learn more. They also help us do our part to protect these unique places and the animals that live there.

Wetland Heroes: Community Conservation Stories

Local Heroes' Tales

Gather around. Let us share inspiring stories. They are about communities who took a stand to protect the wetlands. They are the home of the Fishing Cat. We can find examples of local people who have helped save or fix wetlands that were in trouble. We can tell these stories at a community event or at school.

We can even write them down to show others that when we work together, we can make a significant difference for nature.

Learning About Wetlands Together

Attending or setting up workshops. They will teach us about wetlands and why Fishing Cats are important. They will also show how we can help protect their homes. The workshops can include fun activities. For example, evaluating the water. Also, learning about the plants and who eats whom in the wetlands.

Art and Writing for the Wetlands

Start a writing and art competition. It will be about saving the wetlands and the Fishing Cat. This is a wonderful way to learn and to tell our friends and families why these places are so unique.

Create a Club for Wetland Protectors

Make a club. It is all about caring for our local wetlands and keeping Fishing Cats safe. The club could go on trips to learn more, help with science projects, and speak up for our wetlands.

Meet Real Conservationists

Activity: Invite people who work to save wildlife to come and talk at your school or community group. They can tell us about the challenging work of protecting nature and how every one of us can help.

Help Fix the Wetlands

Activity: Work with groups that care about the environment to help fix wetlands. We might plant new plants. We will get rid of plants that should not be there. We will clean the water. We will learn by doing how we can make these places healthy again.

Hey, young friends! We made these activities to get you excited and involved in taking care of our planet. When you join in, you are not just learning. You are really helping to save the wetlands and the amazing Fishing Cat. Every small thing you do is effective. Together, we can build a world where nature and animals thrive. So put on your explorer hat and let us make a positive change together!

A Salute to the Fishing Cat Moms

Deep in the wetlands of our world, mother Fishing Cats are the watchful keepers of their water homes. These cats have unique swimming feet. They have skills for hunting in the dark. They show us the strength and secrets of the wetlands they live in.

We honor these amazing hunters and caring mothers, and we also promise to do our part to keep their homes safe.

Fishing Cats move through plants and streams. Their lives show how nature is connected. They remind us why we need to take care of it. They face home challenges. They also show us the bigger fight against ruining and losing natural places. Their ability to survive shows us how strong and adaptable nature is. It encourages us to promise to protect our environment.

Let us respect the Fishing Cats and their wetlands. Let us let this respect move us to look after these important places. We have the power to make sure the Fishing Cats and their world can keep doing well. Let us be champions for saving wetlands. Let us celebrate the Fishing Cat moms. They are true guardians of these water-filled lands.

Glossary:

- **Fishing Cat:** A special kind of cat that loves water and is really good at swimming to catch fish.

- **Wetlands:** Wet places like swamps and marshes where lots of animals and plants live.

- **Swimming:** Moving through water. Fishing cats are excellent swimmers, unlike most other cats.

- **Predator:** An animal that hunts other animals for food. Fishing cats are predators that eat fish.

- **Conservation:** The work of protecting animals and their homes from being destroyed.

- **Habitat:** The natural home of an animal. For fishing cats, this includes wetlands and areas near water.

- **Nocturnal:** Animals that are active at night. Fishing cats hunt mostly at night.

- **Camouflage:** Blending in with the environment. Fishing cats' fur helps them hide while hunting.

- **Wetlands in Danger:** Many wetlands are being harmed by pollution and land development, which is bad for fishing cats.

- **Conservation Efforts:** Actions people take to protect animals and their homes, like cleaning up wetlands.

- **Adaptation:** Special features animals have to live in their environments. Fishing cats have webbed feet for swimming.

Part III

Leopard Cat, Flat-Headed Cat, Marbled Cat, Sand Cat, Bobcat, Jungle Cat, and Margay

CHAPTER 15: SHADOWS AND SPOTS: THE LEOPARD CAT'S TALE

Meet the Leopard Cat: A Wild Wonder

The Spotted Forest Cat

In the forests and fields of Asia, there is a small, wild cat called the Leopard Cat.

It has a beautiful coat with spots and moves gracefully and quietly. This little hunter is good at living in many different places. These range from deep green jungles to places near where people live.

A Shy Night Hunter

Leopard Cats like to be on their own and do their hunting at night. They sneak around in the dark, looking for small animals and bugs to eat. They are good at staying hidden. This helps them live in many places, even when things around them change.

Protectors of Nature

These cats are important for the places they live in. By hunting other animals, they help keep everything in balance. Even though we do not see them much, they are a big part of the wild world and show us how everything in nature is connected.

The First Days of a Leopard Cat

A Safe and Cozy Start

When a Leopard Cat mom has kittens, she picks a safe spot hidden away, like a hollow tree or thick bushes. This is where the kittens start their lives, cozy and protected by their mom. She looks after them very well, keeping them warm and fed until they are ready to explore a bit.

Learning About the Wild

As the kittens get older, they start to explore the world outside their den. Their mom teaches them how to move around, hide, and hunt. This time is important because it is when they learn everything they need to live on their own in the wild.

Growing Up in the Forest

Hunting Lessons from Mom

In the quiet of the forest, Leopard Cat moms show their kittens how to hunt. The kittens watch their mom and learn how to sneak up on their food and catch it. They learn about their home and how to stay safe while hunting.

Becoming Wild Cats

The kittens slowly learn how to be good hunters. They practice a lot and start to do things on their own. Their mom watches over them, and when they are ready, they go off to live their own lives as wild cats.

The Life of a Leopard Cat

The Love of a Wild Cat Mom

Leopard Cat moms are very loving and teach their kittens how to survive in the wild. They spend a lot of time with them when they are little, showing them what to do. This time with their mom is important for the kittens because it helps them become strong and smart.

Living Alone in the Wild

When they grow up, Leopard Cats live on their own. They find their own places in the forest and spend their days hunting and taking care of themselves. This is just how they live, and they are exceptionally good at it.

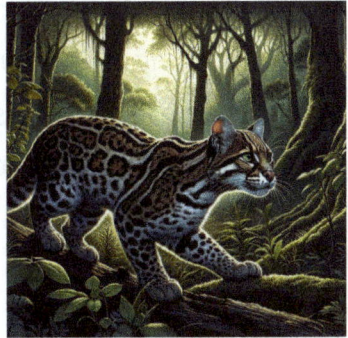

Starting Their Own Families

When they are ready, adult Leopard Cats look for a partner to start their own family. This is how they keep the forest full of Leopard Cats. They pass on everything their mom taught them to their own kittens, keeping the circle of life going in the wild.

The Secret Life of Leopard Cats

Nature's Ninjas

Leopard Cats are experts at hiding. Their spotted fur helps them blend in with the trees and leaves. They move so quietly that they are almost invisible in the forest. They use their sharp eyes and ears to find food and stay safe from bigger animals.

Talking Without Words

Even though they like to be alone, Leopard Cats have their own ways to talk to each other. They make different sounds for different things. They use them for talking to their kittens or finding a mate. They also leave scent marks to tell other cats about their territory. These quiet messages help them live their lives without running into trouble.

Helping Leopard Cats Stay Wild

In Danger

Leopard Cats are facing some big problems. Their homes in the forest are being cut down, and some people try to catch them to sell. This is making it hard for them to find places to live and stay safe.

Conservation Heroes

There are people and groups working hard to keep Leopard Cats safe. They are making laws to protect them. They are fixing up their homes in the forest. They are teaching people about how we can help. These efforts are important to make sure Leopard Cats can keep living wild and free.

Discover the Leopard Cat: A Wild Legacy

Ambassadors of the Wild

Leopard Cats have mysterious ways and are active at night. They are important for keeping nature in balance. They control the number of other small animals. This keeps the environment healthy. These animals are all over Asia. They show the continent's abundant life and the need to care for nocturnal wildlife.

Sharing Our World

The story of the Leopard Cat is a reminder. We need to care for their homes and find ways to live with them. By caring for the forests and fields where these cats live, we ensure they keep going. We also protect the many kinds of life in Asia. Let us work to save these habitats and let Leopard Cats and people live well together.

Fun Ways to Connect with Leopard Cats

Make a Leopard Cat Home

Activity: Build a model of a Leopard Cat's home. Use things from nature to represent where they live, like forests and fields. Add small figures of Leopard Cats and other wild animals. They show how many creatures share their home.

Save the Cats with Your Art

Create posters about Leopard Cats. Show what makes them unique, why they matter, and the dangers they face. Put up your posters at school or share them online to tell more people about how we can help Leopard Cats.

Join a Club to Help Wild Animals

Activity: Be part of a club at school that cares about wild animals. You can plan events, talks, and fundraisers to help save Leopard Cats. You could also invite animal experts to teach us how we can all help protect wild animals.

Teach Others About Leopard Cats

Look up information about Leopard Cats. Make a presentation about where they live, how they act, and how we can keep them safe. Share what you learn with your classmates or family. It will help them understand why it is important to protect these little wild cats.

Write to Help the Cats

Activity: Write letters to groups that work to save the environment. Tell them you care about Leopard Cats and their homes. Ask how you can help and let everyone know why it is important to work together to save wild places.

Clean Up Nature

Activity: Help clean up nature areas near you or start a clean-up day. Even if you have no Leopard Cats where you live. Keeping natural places clean helps all animals and plants. It might inspire people everywhere to care for wildlife homes.

Hey, young friends! By taking part in these activities, you are joining a big adventure to help our planet. Every poster, presentation, and letter are part of a big effort to make things better. Let us get started! By working together, we can make sure Leopard Cats and their wild homes are safe for many years to come.

Living with Leopard Cats

How to Live Together

Leopard Cats and people must live together without problems. This is true when people start living or farming where cats used to roam. We need to understand these challenges to live together in peace. Leopard Cats sometimes come into areas where people live. This can cause problems with pets and farm animals. We need smart ideas to live together without fighting.

Ideas for Peace

To live together peacefully, we need good plans that help both Leopard Cats and people. We can manage their homes by making safe paths for them to move around. We must also make sure they have enough wild animals to eat. This means they will not need to hunt pets or farm animals. We can build safe places for farm animals and help farmers if they lose any animals. Teaching people about Leopard Cats can also help them see the cats differently. It can help them see the cats not as pests, but as important parts of nature. We can make places where both can do well by using smart ideas and sharing stories. The stories are about people and Leopard Cats living together well.

Celebrating the Leopard Cat

In the quiet evenings of Asia, the Leopard Cat moves through the wild. It shows us the beauty and strength of nature. This little hunter has a spotted coat. It represents the spirit of wild places. It lives with the changes around it. Our love for the Leopard Cat is more than just liking how they look. These shy cats remind us how every living thing has a place in nature.

As we finish our story, let us remember to take care of the Leopard Cat and the wild places it lives. We can help make sure these important parts of Asia's nature stay healthy. We can keep the Leopard Cat and all it stands for strong. To do this, people must work together to protect their homes. They must also find ways for animals and people to live together. Let this story inspire us to act. Let us work together to protect the Leopard Cat and its wonderful world.

Glossary:

Leopard Cat: A small wild cat with a beautiful spotted coat, living in Asia's forests and fields.

Night Hunter: Leopard cats hunt at night, using their excellent vision and stealth.

Solitary: Living alone. Leopard cats spend most of their life without company, except for mothers with their kittens.

Conservation: Protecting leopard cats from losing their homes and being hunted.

Habitat: The natural environment where an animal lives. Leopard cats need forests and fields to survive.

Camouflage: The leopard cat's spotted fur helps it hide in its surroundings.

Predator: Leopard cats help control the population of smaller animals and insects.

Threats: The main dangers to leopard cats are habitat destruction and the illegal pet trade.

Adaptation: Leopard cats have adapted to survive in various environments, from jungles to areas near humans.

Ecosystem Role: They play a key role in their ecosystem by maintaining healthy populations of their prey.

Conservation Efforts: Work done by people and organizations to protect leopard cats and their natural habitats.

Wildlife Education: Teaching people about leopard cats and how to protect them and their environments.

CHAPTER 16: MYSTERIES OF THE WATER: THE FLAT-HEADED CAT'S JOURNEY

Introduction to the Flat-headed Cat

A Unique Water Cat

In the jungles of Southeast Asia, there is a unique cat called the flat-headed cat that loves water.

It has webbed feet that help it swim and a flat head that helps it move through water easily. This cat is exceptionally good at swimming

and lives in the forests where there are lots of streams and rivers.

Home in Danger

The flat-headed cat lives in the rainforests. They are found in places like Borneo, Sumatra, and the Malay Peninsula. These forests are important because they give the cat food, a place to live, and a place to have babies. But these forests are in trouble because of cutting down trees and making the water dirty. We need to take care of these rainforests so the flat-headed cat and other animals can survive.

We Need to Protect the Forests

The flat-headed cat's story tells us that we must save the forests and streams where it lives. We should think about how our actions can hurt these places and work to keep them safe. This will help the flat-headed cat and many other animals live there too.

The Flat-headed Cat's Early Days

Safe by the River

Flat-headed cat moms find secret spots by the river to keep their babies safe. They hide their kittens where the plants are thick by the water. The kittens start their lives here, being taken care of by their mom.

Learning to Play in Water

When the kittens are young, they drink their mom's milk and slowly start to see and hear. They learn they can swim, and their mom helps them take their first steps in the water. They play and learn in the water, and their mom watches them quietly. The kittens learn to catch food and become good at living in the water.

Mom Teaches Them Everything

The mom cat teaches her kittens how to live. She shows them how to catch food, stay hidden, and be quiet. As they grow up, they remember everything their mom taught them. This helps them survive by the river.

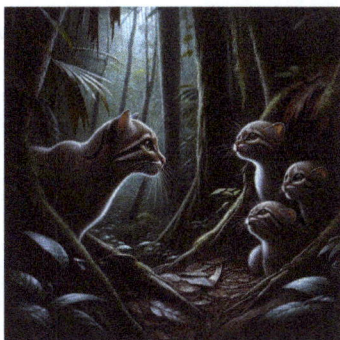

School for Hunting

Learning to Catch Food

The flat-headed cat kittens learn to hunt from their mom. She teaches them how to catch fish, frogs, and bugs. Every time their mom catches something, it is a lesson for the kittens on how to catch their own food one day.

Becoming Independent

The kittens practice catching food and get better at it as time goes by. They learn to be confident and start to do things on their own. The riverbank changes from a classroom with their mom. It becomes a place they can explore alone. They remember their mom's lessons and get ready to live alone as great hunters in their forest home.

From Care to Independence

Caring Cat Moms

Flat-headed cat moms are like superheroes of the jungle. They choose
the safest places for their babies to
live and teach them how to survive.
They show the kittens where to find
food and how to catch it in the water. Thanks to their moms, the kittens
learn everything they need about living in the forest.

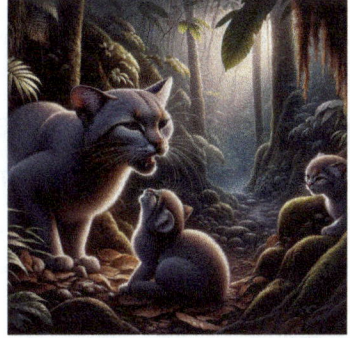

Going Solo

After a while, the kittens must leave their moms and live alone.
Flat-headed cats do not spend time together; each one lives by
itself near the water. They use what their moms taught them to
find food and take care of themselves.

The flat-headed cats start with their mom's help, but they grow
up to live on their own. They use the skills their moms taught
them to live in their own part of the rainforest.

Growing Up by the Water

Mom Is Always Watching

Flat-headed cat moms are always watching their kittens. They
make sure their babies are safe from any danger. Every time
they move to a new place, it is like a lesson for the kittens. The
mom shows them how to live by the river.

Learning to Swim

The mom cat is also the kittens' first teacher. She helps them swim for the first time and teaches them how to catch fish. The kittens learn everything about living in the water from their mom.

Becoming Big Cats

As the kittens grow, they start to do things by themselves. They go from hunting with their mom to hunting alone. They remember their mom's lessons and use them to live by themselves.

Water Wisdom

The flat-headed cat's mom helps them become smart and strong. They learn to hunt and live in the water. When they grow up, they use these skills to survive in the rainforest.

Secrets of the Night

Experts in the Dark

Flat-headed cats are experts at living in the dark. They wake up when the sun goes down and hunt at night. The darkness helps them sneak up on their food. They are hard to see and very mysterious.

Quiet Talks

Even though they are quiet, flat-headed cats have their own ways of talking to each other. Moms talk to their kittens, and they talk to each other when it is time to have babies. They use sounds and smells to communicate in their secret world.

Saving the Cats

In Danger

The flat-headed cat is in trouble because people are changing its home. Their forests are being cut down and their water is getting dirty. We need to act fast to save these cats.

Protectors of the Wetlands

People are working hard to save the flat-headed cats. They make safe places for the cats to live and clean up the water. These projects are important to help the cats survive.

Helping the Ecosystem

The flat-headed cat is important for the health of the forest and water. We need to keep these places safe for all the animals that live there. What happens to the flat-headed cat shows us how the whole ecosystem is doing.

What We Can Do

We can all help save the flat-headed cat and its home. We can clean up rivers, use less water, and choose things that are good for wildlife. We can tell others about how important it is to save these animals and their homes. Let us work together to protect the flat-headed cat and its world.

Getting Involved in Conservation

Make a Model Ecosystem

You can make a model of a wetland where flat-headed cats live. Use things like cardboard and plastic bottles to show the rivers, trees, and animals. This helps us remember to reuse and recycle things.

Clean Up Our Waters

Join or start a day to clean up a river or lake. Learn how pollution hurts the water and the animals. Share what you do with others to teach them about keeping water clean.

Make a Poster

Create a poster about flat-headed cats and the dangers they face. Show how we can help save wetlands. Put your poster up at school or online to tell more people about it.

Watch the Water

Keep a journal about the water near you and the animals you see. Find out why these places are important for animals like the flat-headed cat. Share what you learn with your friends and family.

Talk About Conservation

Get together with friends. You will talk about saving wetlands and animals. For example, the flat-headed cat. You can invite someone who knows a lot about wildlife to tell you more.

Adopt a Cat

Join a program to help save flat-headed cats by raising money. You can do this with your class or family to help organizations that protect animals.

By doing these things, you can be a part of saving our planet. You will learn about nature and how to take care of it. And you will help make sure flat-headed cats and other animals have a home in the future.

Guardians by the Water: The Flat-headed Cat Mom's Gift

A Mom's Gift

The story of the Flat-headed Cat Mom is a powerful one. She starts by protecting her kittens in a safe den and teaches them how to live by the water. Her hard work helps the next group of cats grow up and stay alive in the forest's rivers and streams.

Lessons That Last

She teaches her kittens many things. They include how to follow the river's flow and stay quiet in the bushes. These lessons stay with them as they grow up. Her kittens become great at finding their way around the water, thanks to her. They continue the knowledge she gave them, which helps keep their species going, even when it is hard.

We Must Help

The Flat-headed Cat Mom's story shows us how everything in nature is connected. It tells us we need to take care of the forests and rivers where these cats live. Her strength and care should make us want to look after our planet's unique places. We

should protect the waters that are
home to so much life and respect the cats that live there.

Celebrating the Flat-headed Cat

A Sign of Nature's Beauty

The Flat-headed Cat is amazing. It
shows how nature can change and
make beautiful things. These cats
are like guardians of the rivers and
streams in Southeast Asia's forests.
They have unique body parts that
help them live in the water. By looking
after where they live, we help keep
the balance of life.

A Story of Never Giving Up

The Flat-headed Cat's life is a story of never giving up. It went
from being cared for by its mom to becoming a water expert.
It makes us think about our part in keeping their future safe.
We should do what we can to help our planet's different homes
stay healthy.

We All Have a Part to Play

We finish with a call to all of us to care for our environment.
We keep nature safe by saving the wetlands. We do this by

choosing to live in a way that is good for the planet. We also do this by teaching others about important animals like the Flat-headed Cat.

Let Us Be Guardians Too

Let the Flat-headed Cat's story encourage you to do something. Find out about what is happening to our world's wildlife and speak up to save nature. Let the love these cats have for their water world inspire us to be guardians of the wetlands. We can make sure these places stay alive for a long time.

The Flat-headed Cat is not just an animal; it is a symbol of the life that fills our world. This story is about the beauty and softness of nature. It is also about the lasting spirit of the creatures that live there. We should remember this. We should work to keep the soft sounds of the water telling us about these wonderful cats.

Glossary:

- **Flat-headed Cat:** A unique cat that loves water and has a distinctive flat head, found in Southeast Asia.

- **Rainforests:** Dense, wet forests where flat-headed cats live, rich in biodiversity.

- **Webbed Feet:** Special feet that help the flat-headed cat swim better, like a duck.

- **Endangered:** At risk of disappearing from the wild due to habitat destruction and pollution.

- **Nocturnal:** Active at night, when flat-headed cats do most of their hunting.

- **Ecosystem:** The community of living things in an area, including plants, animals, and microorganisms.

- **Conservation:** Efforts to protect the flat-headed cat and its habitat from further damage.

- **Predator:** An animal that hunts other animals for food. Flat-headed cats mainly eat fish.

- **Habitat Loss:** The main threat to flat-headed cats, as forests are cleared for human use.

- **Adaptation:** Traits that help flat-headed cats live in their watery environments.

- **Protection Efforts:** Actions taken to save flat-headed cats and their rainforest homes.

- **Environmental Awareness:** Teaching people about the importance of protecting flat-headed cats and their ecosystems.

CHAPTER 17: ARBOREAL WHISPERER: THE MARBLED CAT'S SECRET LIFE

Introduction to the Marbled Cat

A Mysterious Tree-Climber

D eep in the green jungles of Southeast Asia, a secretive cat moves through the trees like a ghost.

This is the Marbled Cat, a wildcat with gorgeous fur that twists and turns. It lives high off the ground, hidden in the trees, and is hard to spot.

Home in the High Branches

The Marbled Cat lives in the forests of Borneo, Sumatra, and other parts of Southeast Asia. It spends most of its time in the trees, which give it everything it needs to live. These forests are full of life and are the perfect place for this cat to do its amazing tree-walking tricks. Here are some cool things about the Marbled Cat:

The Marbled Cat has a long tail. It helps it balance when moving through trees. It is like how a tightrope walker uses a pole.

Small but Mighty Hunter:

Even though it is not a big cat, the Marbled Cat is a great hunter. It can grip branches tightly. It can jump around easily. This makes it great for catching food in trees.

Quiet and Sneaky:

The Marbled Cat is so quiet and hard to see that you might only hear a tiny sound or see a little movement. It likes to stay hidden and does not make much noise.

The Marbled Cat shows us how clever nature can be. It is a perfect fit for living in the tree-filled forests and shows us how amazing these places are.

Growing Up in the Trees

Cozy Tree Homes

Baby Marbled Cats, called kittens, are born and live in nests way up in the trees. Their mom picks a safe, snug spot for them to grow up and learn.

Learning to Climb

The little kittens climb and play in the branches early on. Playing is important—it teaches them how to move around the trees without falling. Their mom shows them how to hide and move quietly, which they will need to know for hunting when they get bigger.

Tree Food and Tricks

The kittens get to know their home by learning what they can eat, like bugs and little animals. They also learn to leave marks. The marks show where they have been and help them find their way in their big, leafy world.

Getting Strong and Brave

As they get older, the kittens get better at balancing with their long tails. They also become sure of themselves. Before long, they are ready to go out on their own, with all the tree-living skills their mom taught them.

These first days are super important. They learn not just how to live, but to love life in the trees. They are getting ready for the day they will be grown-up Marbled Cats.

Teaching the Next Wave

Branch Hunting Lessons

In the greenery, Marbled Cat moms show their kittens how to catch prey. These include birds and small animals. This helps the little ones learn to be expert hunters and live in the trees.

Becoming Independent

The kittens practice their hunting and climbing a lot. They get ready for the time when they will go off on their own. They have everything their mom taught them, which is a substantial change.

The lessons are not just about catching food. They are about growing up and being able to care for themselves in the big forest.

Connections in the Canopy

A Mom's Love and Lessons

In the thick leaves, where it is hard to see far, the Marbled Cat mom is the center of her kittens' world. She is not just bringing them food; she is their protector and teacher, showing them how to live in the trees.

Guardian of the Little Ones

The Marbled Cat mom keeps her kittens safe from dangers like other animals that might hurt them. She is always ready to defend them or move them to a safer spot if she needs to.

Teacher of Tree Life

From their first shaky steps on the branches, the kittens learn every-thing from their mom. She shows them how to jump right, stay steady on thin branches, and find their way into their treetop home.

Caring for the Future

The close bond between the mom cat and her kittens is clear in how they play and talk with gentle sounds. Even when they grow up and go their own ways, what their mom taught them will help them for their whole lives.

A Tradition of Caring

The Marbled Cat mom works hard. She ensures her kittens can grow up and keep the Cat family going. They live in the forests of Southeast Asia.

Tree Skills of the Marbled Cat

Born for the Trees

Marbled cats have unique body parts for living in the trees. They have joints that bend easily, sharp claws to hold on tight, and big tails for balance. All this makes them great at climbing and living way up high.

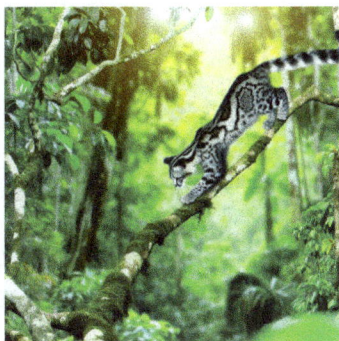

Talking in the Treetops

Marbled cats spend a lot of time by themselves, but they have their own ways of talking to each other. They make unique noises, leave smells, and use body signals to say "hello" or "stay away." This helps them stay in touch in the busy forest.

These cool things about the Marbled Cat show how well it fits into its home in the trees. From the way it moves to how it talks; it is right for life in the forest.

Helping the Forest Stay Alive

A Forest in Trouble

The forests where Marbled Cats live are facing big problems. People are cutting down trees and sometimes even hunting these cats. We need to try hard to protect these forests. They are not important for cats, but for lots of other creatures and plants too.

People Helping

Lots of people are working to help the Marbled Cat and its home. They are making some areas where no one can cut down trees or hunt. They are also trying to stop people from selling these cats. They are planting new trees where forests once were. These actions are important. They ensure Marbled Cats have a home in the future. They also keep the forests of Southeast Asia full of life.

A Symbol of the Wild

The Marbled Cat, hard to find and unique, is a symbol of the wild forests of Southeast Asia. We need to take care of these forests to make sure Marbled Cats and many other creatures can keep living there.

An Invitation to Help

We can all keep the forests healthy. By saving the forests and living in a way that is good for the Earth, we can make sure Marbled Cats will always have a home. Let us all try to take care of the forests so these amazing tree cats can keep whispering through the leaves.

Interactive Exploration

Discover the Forest's Secrets

Learn about the amazing forests where the Marbled Cat lives. Find out what makes tropical forests unique and why it is important to keep them safe. By understanding the forest, we can help protect it and the Marbled Cat too.

Helping from Home

You can help the forests and Marbled Cats even from far away. Talk to people about how important these places are. You can also help by choosing things that do not harm the forest. For example, pick products made from trees grown in an eco-friendly way.

Conclusion: Keeping the Trees Alive

Our adventure with the Marbled Cat is ending, but the story of the forests where they live goes on. These cats are beautiful and full of secrets, just like the jungles they call home.

We have learned that Marbled Cats are strong and can deal with a lot, but they need our help to keep their forests safe. Saving these places means more than just helping one kind of cat. It means taking care of all the different plants and animals that live there.

The Marbled Cat's story reminds us that we all must work together to take care of the forests. By speaking up for the trees and living in a way that does not hurt the planet, we are looking after nature.

Let the quiet sounds of the forest encourage us to keep these places safe. That way, we will make sure the Marbled Cat and all the other creatures in the forest can keep living there. They can live there for a long time to come.

Glossary:

- **Marbled Cat:** A mysterious cat with beautiful, marbled fur, living high in the trees of Southeast Asia.

- **Arboreal:** Living in trees. Marbled cats are excellent climbers and spend most of their life on the branches.

- **Camouflage:** Their unique fur pattern helps them blend into the forest canopy.

- **Conservation:** Protecting marbled cats from threats like deforestation and hunting.

- **Ecosystem:** The complex network of plants, animals, and their environment in the forest.

- **Predator:** Marbled cats are hunters that help control the populations of their prey.

- **Habitat Destruction:** The main danger to marbled cats, as people clear forests for land use.

- **Nocturnal:** Marbled cats are most active at night, hunting and moving through the trees.

- **Adaptation:** Special skills and features that help marbled cats survive in the treetops.

- **Conservation Efforts:** Work by organizations to study marbled cats and protect their forest homes.

- **Biodiversity:** The variety of life in the forest, which marbled cats are a part of.

- **Environmental Education:** Teaching people about the importance of preserving marbled cats and their habitats.

CHAPTER 18: WHISPERS IN THE SAND: THE SAND CAT'S DESERT REALM

Introduction to the Sand Cat: Desert Expert

A Little Desert Hero

In the huge, quiet dunes, a small but amazing animal lives.

This is where the Sand Cat, a true desert expert, calls home. It walks on the hot sand without leaving much of a trace, thanks to fur on its feet. The Sand Cat is great at living in the desert, a place most animals avoid.

The cat's fur looks just like sand and helps it stay hidden from danger. It moves without being seen or heard, but it is always there. Even when the sun is hot, the Sand Cat keeps cool. This shows us how smart nature is to let a cat live well in such a tough place.

Right away, we can see how the Sand Cat fits perfectly with the desert. It lives quietly, but it is an important part of the desert world.

Desert Love Songs

When the Night Comes to Life

When the sun goes down and the desert gets cooler, something unique happens. The usually quiet Sand Cat makes soft noises. These sounds travel through the dunes, helping Sand Cats find each other in the big, empty desert.

A Desert Dance

At night, the Sand Cat moves gracefully, almost melting into the colors of the sand. This time is rare and unique. It shows us how well the Sand Cat can live in one of the toughest places on Earth. Every careful step and quiet sound at night proves they can keep living through tough times in the desert.

Desert School for Kittens

Learning to Live in the Sand

As Sand Cat kittens get bigger, they learn about the desert. Their mom is the best teacher, showing them how to hunt and stay alive. She catches little animals to eat, and the kittens watch to learn how to do it too. But it is more than food—it is about understanding the desert's workings.

The Sand Cat mom also teaches them to listen to the desert sounds and tells them how to find water in their dry home. They learn to get water from the food they eat, which is important for living far from any watery place.

Growing Up and Going Alone

The kittens learn a lot quickly, but soon it is time for them to be on their own. They feel surer, and their senses get better. They still love their mom, but they feel the desert calling them to explore by themselves.

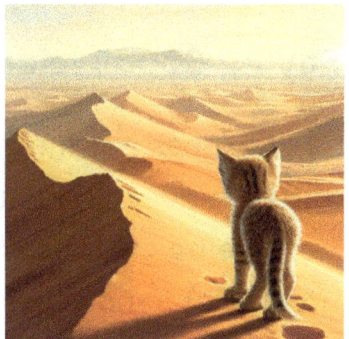

When the time comes to leave, they are ready. The fun playing and watching their mom has taught them everything they need. They are prepared for the desert life, to find their own places, and one day, to teach their own kittens.

Family Ties in the Sand

A Mom's Strong Love

In the desert's heart, the love be-tween a Sand Cat mom and her ba-bies is strong. This is their first les-son in trusting and caring. The mom is always there, keeping them warm in their burrow and helping them learn about the world.

Her lessons are about more than just staying alive. They show the love and strength of the desert. This strong bond helps the kittens grow up to be brave and smart, ready for their desert lives.

Saying Goodbye and Going Solo

As time goes by, things change for the Sand Cat family. The kittens, now grown, must start their own lives. They move from being close to their family to living alone, which is normal for Sand Cats.

Even though they are alone, the love and lessons from when they were little stay with them. Their mom's teachings guide them as they start their own adventures in the desert.

The kittens' journey from their mom's care to being on their own shows how tough and adaptable Sand Cats are. In the big desert, each cat carries on the family legacy, living alone but with a heart full of the love they grew up with.

Secret Skills of the Sand Cat

Desert Ninjas

The Sand Cat is like a ninja in the desert. Its fur matches the sand, so it is hard to see, which helps it stay safe and hunt. They do not just look like the sand; they are also super quiet, which is important for living in the open desert.

The Sand Cat is an expert hunter. It listens for tiny sounds under the sand to find its food. It quickly catches animals despite the limited food in the desert.

Desert Chats

The desert might seem quiet, but Sand Cats have their own way of talking. They make different noises to talk to each other. These sounds are important for finding mates and setting up their home areas. The noises they make help us learn more about how they live and their secret desert life.

Conservation Efforts and Impact: Championing the Sand Cat

Facing the Challenges

The Sand Cat, a small but fierce desert dweller, is under threat. Their homes are disappearing because of human activities like building and changing the land. Another big problem is the illegal pet trade, where people take these wild cats to keep as pets.

Changes in the weather that come with climate change can also hurt the Sand Cats. It can make it harder for them to find food and a good place to live. We need to understand these problems to help the Sand Cats survive.

Defenders of the Desert

People are working hard to save the Sand Cats. They make safe places for the cats, study them to learn more, and instruct people about why it is important to save them.

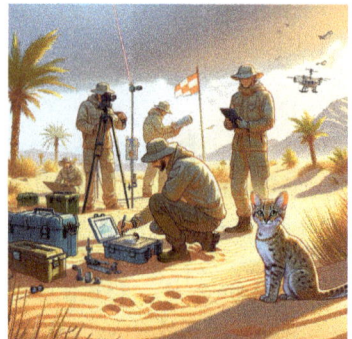

By creating areas where the cats are protected and doing research, we can make better plans to keep them safe. Telling people about the Sand Cats can make more people want to help protect them.

The Sand Cat's Legacy

The Sand Cat is an amazing part of the desert. They help keep their environment healthy by being part of the food chain. Saving these cats also means taking care of the whole desert.

The Sand Cat's story tells us how important it is to take care of nature. Every little thing we do to save the desert helps the whole planet.

Let Us Act

We all can help save the Sand Cats. By learning about them and telling others, we can all be part of keeping Sand Cats safe. Let us work together to take care of the Sand Cats and their desert home.

Desert Harmony: The Sand Cat's Role

The Sand Cat may be a small crea-ture, but it plays a vital role in the delicate balance of the desert ecosystem. By protecting these fur-ry desert animals, we help keep the whole desert healthy. Remember, we should recognize the interconnect-

edness of all living things, regardless
of their size.

Glossary:

- **Sand Cat:** A small, tough cat that lives in the desert, with fur on its feet to protect it from hot sand.

- **Desert:** A dry, sandy environment where sand cats excel in surviving.

- **Nocturnal:** Active at night, which helps sand cats avoid the extreme daytime heat.

- **Conservation:** Efforts to protect sand cats and their desert habitats from threats.

- **Adaptation:** Special traits that help sand cats live in harsh desert conditions.

- **Ecosystem:** The community of living things in the desert, including plants, animals, and insects.

- **Hunting:** Sand cats are predators that eat small animals and insects found in the desert.

- **Endangered:** Sand cats face risks from habitat loss and illegal pet trade.

- **Survival Skills:** Abilities that allow sand cats to find food and water in the desert.

- **Protection Measures:** Actions taken to conserve sand cat populations and their habitats.

- **Environmental Challenges:** Issues like climate change and human expansion that threaten sand cats.

- **Awareness and Education:** Teaching people about the importance of sand cats and how to protect them.

CHAPTER 19 - BOBCAT CHRONICLES: THE RESILIENT MOMS OF THE WILD

Welcome to the World of Bobcats

Amazing Adapters

S ay hello to the bobcat, a super cool animal that can live in many places in North America.

Whether it is a thick forest or a dry desert, the bobcat knows how to survive and find food. They are good at living in various places. This makes them interested in learning about and watching.

Speckled Hiders

Bobcats have fur with spots that help them blend in with their home. They are so good at hiding that some people call them "speckled hiders." They can stay out of sight, which is great when they are hunting. It is also why bobcats are such a mystery and why people care about keeping them safe.

Icons of the Wild

Bobcats are important animals in North America. They help keep nature in balance by eating other animals and helping plants grow. They are also a big part of stories and efforts to protect wild animals. Bobcats really show the free spirit of North America's outdoors.

New Bobcat Babies

Safe Baby Bedrooms

Momma bobcats pick secret places to have their babies. They might choose a thick bush or a spot under rocks to keep their little ones safe from danger and severe weather. These hiding places are perfect for keeping the baby bobcats safe. The bobcats use

these hiding places while they are small.

Little Ones' First Look

Baby bobcats are born blind and need their momma's warmth and milk to grow. They start to grow quickly. They also begin to explore the world near them, always with their mom keeping a close eye on them.

Learning and Playing

As the baby bobcats get older, they start to play and pretend to fight. This is how they learn important skills when they grow up. Their momma takes loving care of them and teaches them everything they need to know.

Teaching the Babies

Hunting School

Momma bobcats teach their kids how to hunt when they are still young. The babies watch and learn how to move quietly, follow animals they want to catch, and know the best time to jump on them. This is how they learn to find their own food.

Play Turns into Practice

The baby bobcats' play fights and chasing games become real hunting lessons. They get better at moving around and catching animals quietly. They are like grown-up bobcats.

Growing Up

The baby bobcats try to hunt on their own, with their momma showing them how. This helps them get ready for the day when they will leave their momma and find their own place to live.

Bobcat Families

Learning to Be Alone

Bobcats usually live by themselves, and this starts when they are babies. Momma bobcats teach their babies how to do well on their own, which is important for living in the wild.

Getting Ready to Leave

Bobcat babies slowly start doing more things without their momma's help. They go from hunting together to making their first catch by themselves. This time is important because they learn to take care of themselves and become adults.

Remembering Family

Even though bobcats live alone, they never forget the bond with their momma when they were little. This early time is full of learning and growing. It helps them become successful hunters on their own. These lessons are important for keeping the bobcat family going strong.

Bobcats: Cool Creatures of the Wild

What Bobcats Eat

Bobcats can eat lots of different animals, depending on where they live. They can catch speedy mice or even deer. Being good at finding various kinds of food helps nature stay balanced and healthy.

How Bobcats Talk

Bobcats might be hard to spot, but they have their own ways to talk to each other. They make quiet noises and use body language. This helps them instruct their babies and keep their home safe.

Bobcats Are Sneaky

Bobcats are like ninjas of the wild. They walk without making a sound and their fur helps them hide. This sneakiness lets them surprise their dinner and stay away from bigger animals.

Growing Up Bobcat

Becoming Big Cats

Bobcat babies grow up to live by themselves. They learn to hunt and do everything on their own, thanks to their mom teaching them well.

Learning to Live Alone

Bobcat babies practice how to live alone while they are still with their mom. She teaches them to hunt, find their way, and mark their space. This time is important for them to learn how to be grown-ups in the wild.

Finding New Home

When bobcat babies are ready, they leave their family to find their own place. This big step is full of adventures and helps keep the bobcats going.

Helping Bobcats Stay Safe

Taking Care of Bobcats

Bobcats are doing okay, but they need safe places to live without too much human stuff in the way. People are working to keep the land safe for bobcats. They make rules to protect them and teach everyone about these cool cats.

Bobcats Keep Nature Happy

Bobcats help a lot by eating other animals and making sure there are not too many. This helps all the plants and animals live well together. Saving bobcats means saving lots of other living things too.

Working Together for Bobcats

Saving bobcats is a team effort. Wildlife groups, people who care about nature, and everyone else can help. We can all do our part to make sure bobcats stay around.

Bobcat Moms Are Amazing

Teaching the Little Ones

Bobcat moms are great at showing their kittens how to survive in the wild. This helps the baby bobcats get ready to live on their own adventures.

Symbols of Being Tough

Bobcat moms show us how to be strong and handle different situations. They take care of their babies and teach us about nature's power.

Remembering Bobcat Lessons

What bobcat moms teach their kittens helps keep the wild places full of life. These lessons are important for keeping everything in nature working right.

Fun Bobcat Activities

Make Your Own Bobcat Den

Build a bobcat den with boxes, leaves, and sticks to learn about where these animals live.

Story Time with Bobcats

Draft a fun story or draw a comic about a young bobcat's day. Talk about its playtime, learning, and adventures.

Art for Bobcats

Create a beautiful poster that shows how cool bobcats are and tells people how to help them. You can put up your poster for others to see and learn from.

Be a Bobcat Buddy

Join a group or start a project to help people learn about bobcats. You can clean up a park or plant trees to make the world better for wildlife.

Discover Bobcat Secrets

Go on a scavenger hunt to find out fun facts about bobcats. Share what you learn with your friends and family.

Create Bobcat Art

Draw, paint, or make digital art inspired by bobcats and their homes. Show your artwork to others to teach them about these impressive animals.

You Can Be a Hero for Bobcats

Be a Wildlife Champion

You can be a hero like bobcat moms by learning about animals and their homes. Share what you know and get creative with projects about bobcats.

Your Wildlife Hero Mission

Help keep our planet clean and safe for animals. Join a club, plant trees, or clean up a park. Even trivial things can make a significant difference.

Talk About Protecting Wildlife

Tell people why it is important to take care of animals like bobcats. Share your projects and ideas with everyone you know.

Let Us Take Care of Our World Together

Just like bobcat moms take care of their kittens, we can take care of our planet. When we learn, share, and act, we help more than just bobcats—we help our entire world. Let us be guardians of the wild together!

Glossary:

- **Bobcat:** A wild cat with a short tail and spotted fur that lives in many places in North America.

- **Adapters:** Animals that can live in different environments, like forests or deserts.

- **Speckled Hiders:** Nickname for bobcats because of their ability to blend into their surroundings.

- **Kittens:** Baby bobcats, born blind and dependent on their mom.

- **Hunting School:** How momma bobcats teach their kittens to hunt.

- **Independence:** When young bobcats learn to live and hunt on their own.

- **Conservation:** Efforts to protect bobcats and their natural habitat.

- **Ninjas:** Describes how bobcats are stealthy and skilled hunters.

- **Family Ties:** The connection between bobcat mothers and their kittens.

Chapter 20: Master of the Grasslands: The Jungle Cat's Untold Story

The Jungle Cat: Master of Open Space

Meet the Jungle Cat, a unique cat that is not from the jungle at all!

It loves to live in places like semi-deserts, wetlands, and big grassy fields. It has a sleek body, long legs, and a short tail—all perfect for life in these different spots.

A Cat with Many Homes

The Jungle Cat might have "jungle" in its name, but it prefers lots of space to roam. It can be happy in Egypt's sandy areas or the wide grassy lands of Southeast Asia, fitting in wherever it goes.

Unique Jungle Cat Traits

What is cool about the Jungle Cat? Its ears have black tips that help it hear far away sounds. This cat is also not afraid of getting wet—it can swim and catch fish with a quick jump!

Nature's Helper

The Jungle Cat is super important for keeping nature nice and balanced. It hunts animals like mice and helps make sure they do not eat too many plants or crops.

Baby Jungle Cats' Secret Start

Cozy Hidden Homes

Jungle Cat moms find secret places to
have their babies. They might use a
thick bunch of plants or an old burrow another animal made. These hidden spots are where the kittens begin
their lives, safe and warm.

Guardian Moms

The mom protects her kittens in their hidden home and starts
teaching them about life in the wild. This is where they learn
all the important things they need to know.

Kitten Classroom

Right from when they first open their eyes, the mom teaches
the kittens how to be sneaky and quiet. They practice sneaking
up on things and listening to all the surrounding sounds.

Learning to Hunt and Grow Up

Hunting Lessons

Jungle Cat kittens go on big learning adventures with their
mom. She teaches them how to hunt different animals. They
practice a lot to get good at it.

Road to Being Grown-Ups

As the kittens get bigger, they get more confident. They slowly start doing things on their own, getting ready for the day they will have to live by themselves.

Family Life of Jungle Cats

Strong Family Ties

Jungle Cat moms and their kittens have a strong bond. The mom teaches them everything they need to survive and grow up strong.

Alone but Sometimes Together

Jungle Cats usually live alone. But they meet up with others sometimes, like during mating season. Moms and their kittens have a lot of fun together, learning and playing.

Jungle Cat Survival Skills

Swimming and Nighttime Activities

Jungle Cats are wonderful swimmers and like to be active at night or in the early morning. This helps them find food in various places.

Talking and Living Alone

Jungle Cats make different sounds to talk to each other. They have unique noises for finding a mate or telling others to stay away. These sounds help them live in their own space.

Jungle Cats are good at living in all sorts of places. They have lots of skills that help them adapt and be happy wherever they are.

The Jungle Cat's Fight for Home

The Jungle Cat, known for its ability to adapt and be strong, is facing tough times. Their homes are being broken up because people are building more farms and cities. Sometimes they get into trouble when looking for food on farms, and people might catch them to keep as pets. The problems are different in each place they live, from Egypt to South-

east Asia. But everywhere, people are trying to help these amazing cats survive.

Heroes of the Habitats

The health of grasslands and wet-lands around the world depends on keeping Jungle Cats safe. These places are home to lots of different animals, not just the Jungle Cat. Laws protect these areas. There are projects to fix damaged habitats. There are programs to help humans and an-imals live together. We care for these places. It keeps our world beautiful and helps the Jungle Cat and many other animals live well.

The Jungle Cat as a Wild Leader

The Jungle Cat is more than just a cat; it is a leader for the open spaces it lives in, like riverbanks and grasslands. It helps keep nature in balance, which is why we need to look after these places. We must make sure the Jungle Cat and the natural world we all need can keep going strong.

Living Together in Peace

The story of the Jungle Cat is about finding ways for people and animals to live together. We need to find smart ways to stop fights and keep nature safe. We can make a world where the Jungle Cat and other animals can live without problems. We do this by using wildlife paths and farming carefully.

Jungle Cat Adventures

Get to Know Their World

You can learn a lot about Jungle Cats by making a model of where they live or by helping with wildlife projects. Find out how important grasslands and wetlands are for animals like the Jungle Cat.

Speak Up for the Jungle Cat

You can help the Jungle Cat by supporting groups that protect animals and their homes. Every little thing you do helps the Jungle Cat. For example, being kind to wildlife or making excellent rules for nature.

Learn Cool Jungle Cat Facts

Did you know that Jungle Cats can jump high to catch birds? Or that they are great swimmers, which is rare for cats? They can live in deserts and wet places because they are so tough. When you tell people these fun facts, they will care about Jungle Cats just as much as you do.

Hope for the Grasslands

The Quiet Cat of the Fields

The Jungle Cat is a quiet but powerful symbol of nature's open lands. Learning about them from when they are small to when they grow up shows us how important it is to keep nature safe.

Working Together for Nature

The Jungle Cat's life tells us we all need to help protect the world. We must take care of the places that are important for all animals. Keeping nature safe is a big job, but it is something we can do together.

Be Part of the Story

We all have a part to play in taking care of nature because of the Jungle Cat. By joining local efforts, we protect homes for animals. This makes the future brighter for all creatures. Sharing the story of the Jungle Cat can inspire everyone. It can make them want to keep our planet's grasslands and wetlands safe.

A Future Full of Life

The story of the Jungle Cat is a powerful reminder of the beauty and strength of nature. These amazing cats show us how to face challenges and keep the balance of life. By telling their story. We can get everyone excited about protecting the wide-open spaces they call home. Let us make sure the Jungle Cat's story helps us save the wild and wonderful world we all share.

Glossary:

Jungle Cat: A wild cat that prefers living in grasslands and wetlands, not jungles.

Semi-deserts: Dry areas with little water, where jungle cats can also live.

Unique Traits: Special characteristics, like the jungle cat's long legs and ability to swim.

Ecosystem Services: The benefits that nature provides, like hunting by jungle cats that helps control rodent populations.

Conservation: Actions taken to protect jungle cats and their habitats.

Adaptation: How jungle cats adjust to living in different environments.

Habitat Fragmentation occurs when human activities break up the places where jungle cats live.

Coexistence: Finding ways for humans and jungle cats to live together in peace.

CHAPTER 21 - MARGAY MELODIES: THE ELUSIVE MOTHERS OF THE TREETOPS

Discovering the Margay: Magical Tree Dweller

Morning in the Treetops

When the sun rises and the rainforest wakes up, there is a unique cat called the Margay getting ready to start its day. This amazing animal lives up in the trees where it moves quietly and gracefully, just like the mist in the early morning.

The Margay's Tree Home

Margay loves to climb and jump around the branches, and it is good at it. Its beautiful fur looks just like the sun and shadows in the leaves, helping it hide from other animals. This rainforest is where the Margay is in charge, leaping from tree to tree like it is nothing!

The Rainforest's Secret

If you listen closely, you can feel the magic of the Margay. This cat is a wild and beautiful part of the forest, moving around so quietly that you might not even know it is there.

New Margay Kittens High Up

A Nest in the Trees

Deep in the rainforest, a mother Margay picks the perfect spot in a tree to have her babies. It is safe and hidden, a cozy nest high above the ground where her little kittens will take their first breaths.

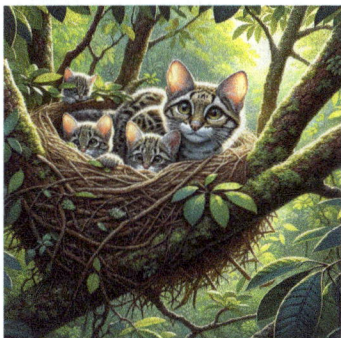

Learning to Climb

The baby Margays start their life sur-
rounded by the sounds and warmth of
the rainforest. They play and learn how
to balance, climb, and move just like
their mom, getting ready for the day
they will be big cats in the trees.

Growing Up in the Rainforest

Nature's Playground

The Margay mom has a lot to teach her kittens, and the trees
are their classroom. They learn to move quietly and jump
far, turning playtime into important lessons for living in the
rainforest.

Quiet Hunters

Margays are great at hunting without making a sound, catching their
food easily. They use their long tails
to keep their balance and move
quickly through the trees, even at
night.

The Margay's Hidden World

The Margay has some unique skills that make it perfect for
living in the treetops. It can balance with its tail, talk to oth-

er Margays in the dark, and hunt without being seen. These amazing things help Margay live a secret life in the rainforest.

Becoming a Grown-Up Margay

First Solo Adventures

As the Margay kittens grow, they become stronger and smarter. They learn to climb and hunt on their own, getting ready for the day they will leave their mom and find their own place in the rainforest.

Saying Goodbye

When it is time, the young Margays leave their mom to start their own adventures. They take with them all the lessons they have learned about living on the treetops.

A Story of the Wild

The life of a Margay, from a little kitten to a grown-up cat, is a beautiful story of growing up and learning to survive in the wild. It is a reminder of how unique the rainforest is and why we need to take care of it and all the creatures that call it home.

Our Rainforest Responsibility

The Enchanting Margay's Challenge

The Margay is a magical animal that moves through the trees of Central and South American rainforests. But this incredible cat and its home are in trouble because of things like cutting down trees and climate change. We all need to help protect Margay and the other animals that live in the rainforest.

Small Steps for Big Change

Even if you are young, you can still do a lot to help the Margay and the rainforest:

1. **Learn and Tell Others:** Find out more about the Margay and why it is important to save rainforests. Then tell your friends and family what you have learned.

2. **Help Conservation Groups:** There are lots of people working to protect the Margay and its home. You can help by giving a little money or joining in their projects.

3. **Make Good Choices:** Use less, recycle, and pick products that are good for the environment. You can make a

significant difference by doing simple things every day.

4. **Speak Up:** Let people know that you care about the rainforest. You can write letters, help clean up your neighborhood, or join events that help the planet.

5. **Grow a Tree:** Planting trees helps make the air cleaner and the earth greener. Every tree you plant helps the Margay and other animals.

A Promise for the Future

By taking care of the rainforest, we are making sure that the Margay can keep leaping through the trees. Every little thing we do adds up to a big promise to look after our planet.

Mother Margay's Love

Just like human moms, mother Margays show their babies how to live in the rainforest. This unique bond is all about love and teaching important lessons for life.

Thanking Mothers Everywhere

Margay's story reminds us to say thank you to our moms. They teach us, love us, and help us grow up to be the best we can be.

Taking Care of Our World

Margay's story is about more than just a cat—it is about all of us taking care of the world. We can learn from mother Margays and do our part to protect the earth.

Listening to the Rainforest

Margay's story ends with a simple idea: listen to the sounds of nature. Whether you are in a rainforest or your own backyard, there is an entire world to discover if you just pay attention.

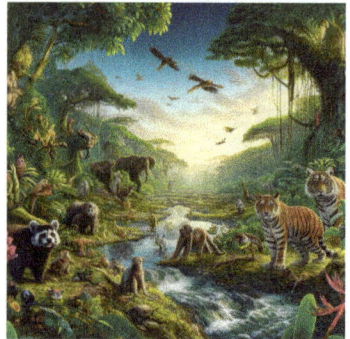

Nature's Beautiful Music

Take a moment to enjoy the nature around you. From the wind in the trees to the birds in the sky, every sound is a part of life's amazing story.

Our Role in Nature

We are all connected to nature, and we all have a part to play in keeping it safe. Even trivial things, like planting flowers or saving water, can help a lot.

Caring for Our Home

Margay's life in the trees shows us how important it is to look after our planet. By being mindful and acting, we can make sure that the earth's beauty and wonder are here for everyone to enjoy, now and in the future.

Glossary:

- **Margay:** A small, tree-dwelling wild cat with a beautiful coat, living in Central and South American rainforests.

- **Arboreal:** Living in trees, like the margay does.

- **Kittens:** Baby margays that learn to climb and hunt in the trees.

- **Rainforest:** A dense, wet forest where margays live, full of life and diversity.

- **Conservation:** Efforts to protect margays and their rainforest home.

- **Hunting Techniques:** The ways margays catch their

prey, using stealth and agility.

- **Deforestation:** Cutting down trees in the rainforest, a threat to margays.

- **Biodiversity:** The variety of life in the rainforest, including margays.

- **Eco-friendly Choices:** Actions people can take to help protect the environment and animals like the margay.

- **Rainforest Magic:** The unique and mysterious beauty of the rainforest, home to the margay.

BENEATH THE SAME SKY

A FAREWELL WITH PURPOSE

As we gaze once more into the endless sky, our journey through the lives of extraordinary cat moms ends. Together, we have discovered the courage, love, and wisdom that bind the tapestry of nature. Every creature, from the majestic lioness to the stealthy snow leopard, plays a vital role in this intricate web of life.

Our adventure may end, but the mission remains: to safeguard the homes of these remarkable beings. It is a big task, but united, we can be effective. Cherish our shared memories and let them inspire actions that protect our planet and its wild wonders.

Thank you for joining me on this voyage of discovery. May your curiosity and kindness continue to grow, and remember, whenever you wish to revisit our adventures or share new ones, I am just a thought away. Keep exploring, cherish our natural world, and look to the sky with hope and wonder. Farewell, my young friends, until our paths cross again under the vast, beautiful sky.

Warmest wishes,

Your friend, The Sky.

Mr. Sky's Feline Fact Files

Question #1: Why can't snow leopards roar like other big cats?

Mr. Sky Explains: Snow leopards cannot roar. Their throats are different, so they are the silent whisperers of the mountains!

Question #2: How do cheetahs achieve their incredible speed?

Mr. Sky Explains: Cheetahs are the sprinters of the animal kingdom. This is thanks to their flexible spine and long legs. The legs act like powerful springs!

Question #3: What unique features do fishing cats have that help them swim?

Mr. Sky explains: The water acrobats of the feline kingdom, fishing cats, have webbed paws!

Question #4: Why do lions live in groups called prides?

Mr. Sky explains: Lions stick together in pride to hunt better and protect each other. Teamwork makes the dream work in the savannah!

Question #5: How do bobcats adapt to different habitats across North America?

Mr. Sky explains that bobcats are the chameleons of the cat world. They have a flexible diet and a coat that blends into both forests and deserts!

Question #6: What unique adaptation helps the Canadian lynx hunt in deep snow?

Mr. Sky Explains: The Canadian lynx has huge paws. They work like natural snowshoes. They let the lynx chase dinner without sinking!

Question #7: How do ocelots mark their territory?

Mr. Sky Explains: Ocelots are the graffiti artists of the jungle, using scent marks to say, "Keep out!" to others.

Question #8: What's the secret behind the leopard's spotted coat?

Mr. Sky Explains: Leopards wear spots to blend into the light and shadows of the forest. This makes them masters at hiding when stalking prey.

Question #9: Why are margays known as the acrobats of the cat world?

Mr. Sky Explains: Margays can rotate their ankles 180 degrees. This lets them climb down trees headfirst and leap through the air with ease!

Question #10: How does the sand cat survive without water in the desert?

Mr. Sky Explains: Sand cats are desert survivors. They get all their water from their prey. They do not need a water bottle!

Question #11: How do tigers use their stripes?

Mr. Sky explains: Tigers have unique stripes. They help tigers blend into the forest and be invisible to their prey. It is like their own set of jungle pajamas!

Question #12: How do cougars manage to be such silent hunters?

Mr. Sky Explains: Cougars have big, strong paws. They have soft padding, which lets them move through the forest as silently as whispers. This makes them stealthy hunters, sneaking up on their prey like ninjas of the animal kingdom!

Question #13: How do caracals use their ears to hunt?

Mr. Sky Explains: Caracals have long, tufted ears that help them hear prey from far away. It is like having built-in radar dishes on their heads!

Question #14: Why do servals have such large ears?

Mr. Sky Explains: Servals use their oversized ears to detect tiny movements in the grass. They can hear a mouse's heartbeat from several feet away!

Question #15: What makes the African golden cat so elusive?

Mr. Sky Explains: The African golden cat is an expert in stealth, living deep in the rainforest where few humans go. They are the secret agents of the feline world!

Question #16: How do Pallas's cats survive in the cold steppes of Central Asia?

Mr. Sky Explains: Pallas's cats have thick fur and a stocky body to keep warm. They are the fluffy marshmallows of the cat kingdom, built for cuddling… if only they were not so wild!

Question #17: What is unique about the jaguar's bite?

Mr. Sky explains: Jaguars have a powerful bite. It is strong enough to pierce turtle shells and skulls. They are the ultimate can openers of the animal kingdom!

Question #18: Why are snow leopards' tails so long?

Mr. Sky explains: Snow leopards have long, fluffy tails. They use them to keep their balance on rocky cliffs and to wrap around themselves for warmth. It is their personal blanket and balance pole!

Question #19: How do Eurasian lynxes cope with deep snow?

Mr. Sky explains: Eurasian lynxes have big paws. They spread their weight, so they can walk on snow without sinking. They are the snowshoe enthusiasts of the wild!

Question #20: Why do cheetah cubs have a mantle of fur on their backs?

Mr. Sky Explains: Cheetah cubs have a mantle of fur. It mimics a honey badger, making them look scarier to predators. It is their version of wearing a superhero cape!

Question #21: How does the Caracal catch birds in flight?

Mr. Sky Explains: The Caracal is known for its great agility and strong hind legs. It uses them to leap high and catch birds from the sky. This impressive "fifth limb" ability shows that Caracal is a skilled hunter. It uses precision, timing, and athleticism to catch its avian prey mid-flight. Truly, the Caracal is the high jumper of the feline world, making it a spectacular sight in the hunt.

ABOUT THE AUTHOR

Shiva Kumar begins his literary adventure with "Caring Claws: The World of Cat Moms," fulfilling a dream over a decade in the making. An IT professional by trade, Shiva's roots trace back to India, though he has called the United States home since 2000. He is transitioning from the structured world of technology to the boundless realms of fiction and non-fiction. This move highlights his belief in the power of evolution and self-realization.

For years, the idea of writing simmered in the back of his mind, a silent whisper of potential that he hesitated to explore. Yet, as the landscape of publishing transformed, so too did his resolve. Digital tools and platforms advanced. They became the bridge between his dreams and reality. They let him weave the complex stories and insights that had long filled his mind.

"Caring Claws" is not just a book; it is a testament to Shiva's passion for the natural world and its most enigmatic inhabitants. It's a leap from the familiar to the unknown. A deep desire to share his fascination with the wild and its lessons on resilience, care, and the complexity of parental bonds motivates him.

Shiva's journey from dreaming to doing is an encouragement to all aspiring writers. The time is now, and we have the tools to turn visions into creations. Through "Caring Claws," Shiva invites readers to explore the untold stories of the animal kingdom. The book opens doors to understanding and empathy that go beyond boundaries and species.

Shiva welcomes thoughts, questions, and connections from readers. Reach out to him at crimsonsummitinc@outlook.com to share your experiences or just to say hello.